Massage
for Cyclists

Massage

for Cyclists

Roger Pozeznik

VITESSE PRESS

Massage For Cyclists

Published by Vitesse Press
PMB 367, 45 State Street
Montpelier, Vermont 05601-2100

ISBN 0-94150-33-6

Library of Congress card number 95-61678

Cover, text design and diagrams by James Brisson
Photos by Bob Tindle

Manufactured in the United States of America

Distributed in the United States by Alan C. Hood, Inc. (717-267-0867)

For sales inquiries and special prices for bulk quantities, contact Vitesse Press at 802-229-4243 or write to the address above.

THIS BOOK IS DEDICATED

IN MEMORY OF

ERICKA

CONTENTS

The winning touch

by Edmund R. Burke

European coaches and cyclists have long appreciated the merits of massage, incorporating it regularly in their training and competition schedules. But massage has traditionally been misrepresented and misunderstood in North America. This is unfortunate because massage can be one of the techiniques that separates elite cyclists from the less than elite.

The integrated cyclist – simultaneously aware of body, mind, and spirit – tends to perform better than the fragmented being. When combined with proper training, balanced nutrition, and a positive attitude, massage can be an excellent conditioning, psychological, and recovery tool.

Chris Carmichael, National Coaching Director for the U.S. Cycling Team, says of his experiences with massage: "Prior to and during this year's World Championships, without the use of massage and competent medical care, our athletes would not have done as well. It relaxes the muscles, particularly after heavy training when they feel completely spent. It helps them relax and fully recover."

The benefits attributed to massage are so many and varied that it's no wonder it's become one of the tools necessary to train properly and compete. Though many cyclists are still learning about these benefits, more and more of them are using massage to enhance their training, improve performance, and help solve muscle problems.

Muscle maintenance

Massage during training is said to help cyclists recover faster from intense training and to increase training potential. Regular massage makes for healthier muscles. More technically, manual massage aids the venous and lymphatic return and prevents stasis in the capillaries of the muscles. There is an increase of blood flow as well as an increase in the interchange of substances between the blood and the tissue cells. Secondary effects include an increase in peripheral blood flow and a decrease in the swelling of muscle cells. In general, massage is used for relief of pain, relaxation of muscle tension, improvement of circulation, reduction of swelling, and to help stretch the muscles.

Massage will not directly increase the strength of normal muscles. But it is more effective than rest in promoting recovery from the fatigue produced by excessive cycling. Massage can help maintain the muscles in the best possible state of health, flexibility, and vitality so that after recovery from a hard ride they can function at their maximum potential.

Pre-competition massage

Massage before competition theoretically increases or decreases the excitability of the nerve cells — depending on the type, duration, and intensity of the massage. In addition, massage proponents say it warms the muscles, joints, and ligaments, thus protecting against micro-injury.

This type of massage focuses on stretching and warming up the ligaments and tendons of the limbs. Connective tissue doesn't have its own blood supply, so it tends to warm up more slowly than muscle. Relaxed muscle allows for more blood flow to the muscles, tendons and ligaments. It also helps calm down the cyclist afflicted with pre-race anxiety and muscle tension.

It's best to begin this massage before the warm-up on the bike. Slow stroking should be used for calming and relaxing the athlete and a kneading, tapping, or vibrating stroke for stimulating and warming the muscles. Follow the massage with some stretching and normal warm-up procedures.

Post-competition massage

A post-event massage helps eliminate the effects of fatigue. It reduces soreness and tension in muscles, while maintaining flexibility and elasticity in the muscles, tendons, and ligaments. Restorative massage after competition is said to speed muscle recovery two to three times faster than passive rest, because it promotes blood and lymph flow. It may even help remove lactic acid if it occurs within the first 15 to 20 minutes after exercise.

During hard cycling, microtrauma occurs in the muscle cells. In addition, there is a bit of swelling of the muscle tissue, and massage helps reduce this. Usually a combination of deep longitudinal strokes to stimulate blood flow, jostling or shaking to relax the muscle, and cross-fiber massage is used to prevent build-up of adhesions, relieve pain and stiffness, and smooth out trigger points that have flared up due to training or racing.

A few years ago a study was done at the Karolinska Institute in Stockholm on the effects of massage on competitive cyclists after they pedaled to exhaustion. Half the group then rested for ten minutes, the other half received ten minutes of massage. They were then asked to do 50 knee extensions on an exercise machine that tested leg strength. The researchers found that leg quadriceps muscles of the massaged cyclists averaged 11 percent stronger than those of the cyclists that rested for ten minutes.

A complete massage after a hard race will take at least 30 minutes and should leave the cyclist feeling physically and psychologically improved. Massage should be done in the evening, about one to one-and-a-half hours after the evening meal. This will leave time for the meal to be partially digested so more blood can be directed to the muscles.

Injury repair

For cyclists with injuries, massage can provide a greater range of movement and help speed the healing process in the injured muscle. In addition, it can help reduce the emotional stress that comes with inactivity. However, Andy Pruitt, director of sports medicine for the U.S. Cycling Team, cautions that massage must be used with care if there is muscle damage or any acute injury with swelling. Under these conditions, he says, "massage would only traumatize the injured area further." Massage should not be applied to the injured tissue for 48 to 72 hours after the initial trauma or until the swelling and pain have substantially subsided. The three main contraindications to massage are deep muscle trauma, surface abrasions, and tendinitis.

By increasing blood and lymph movement, massage increases nutrition to joints and muscles while hastening the elimination of swelling and inflammatory waste products in the muscles. The primary ways that lymph moves through the body is through deep breathing, muscular movement, or massage. Massage pressure can help stimulate the lymphatic vessels when exercise is impossible. Massage helps maintain muscle tone and can help delay muscular atrophy resulting from time off the bicycle.

Massage feels good

Nothing feels better to an athlete after a hard training session or race than a professional massage therapist's warm, oil-covered hands kneading and stroking the athlete's legs and back. The muscles become looser and looser, and the massage therapist's fingers probe deeper and deeper. The more pliable the muscles become, the more exquisite the state of relaxation.

After a hard session, the therapist works systematically, progressing from feet to legs to lower back to shoulders, until all the knots and kinks have been worked out and the athlete's body feels relaxed.

It's clear that the hands-on approach tells athletes that someone understands their problems and pain. This is extremely helpful in the healing process. Touching the skin has an effect on the sensory nerves, which gives cyclists a sense of well-being.

It's been said that the race is not always to the swift but to those who keep cycling. Sports massage helps eliminate the effects of fatigue, both physically and psychologically, while restoring life to the muscles and reducing the possibility of injury. It is also an incredible recuperative tool for injured athletes.

Exercise and sports physiologist Edmund R. Burke, Ph.D., at the time of his death in 2003, was a professor and the director of the exercise science program at the University of Colorado at Colorado Springs. He served as a consultant to USA Cycling, was manager of the 1980 U.S. Olympic Cycling Team and a staff member of the 1984 Olympic cycling effort. He wrote or edited 16 books and contributed frequently to several popular cycling magazines.

Massage *for* Cyclists

Cycling can be a strenuous sport. Whether you ride just for fun, train regularly for fitness, or compete at any level, you want to get the most from your muscles. Massage can help you do that.

Professional cycling teams and other athletes have been reaping the benefits of massage for many years. Now you can too. The techniques you'll learn in this book are designed to help you prepare for and recover from exercise.

The pre-ride massage works to wake and warm up your legs before getting on the bike. You'll feel looser and less sore when you start riding, which means you'll enjoy your on-bike warm-up more and be less likely to injure yourself.

After a ride, massage speeds along the removal of the waste products of exercise, helping you recover sooner, with less soreness. For most people, the post-ride massage is relaxing, both mentally and physically, and contributes to better sleep, which can be just as important as the workout.

As a sports massage therapist and an athlete, I'm often asked about effective ways to relieve muscle soreness and reduce injury. This book is my answer. With regular use, the basic massage skills will help to improve your performance, decrease your recovery time, and minimize your aches and pains.

Good luck with your new skills! I think you'll be amazed to discover the powers of touch, through sports massage.

How to use this book

I have designed this book to be visual. I've tried to use as few technical terms as possible, to keep it readable and interesting.

The print is large so you can lay the book down and refer to it as you're working. The pictures show the techniques, with captions to reinforce what you're doing.

There are two photos for every massage stroke, one (left) showing how it starts and one (right) how it finishes. By looking quickly from one to the other, you should be able to visualize the motion.

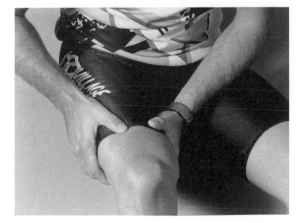 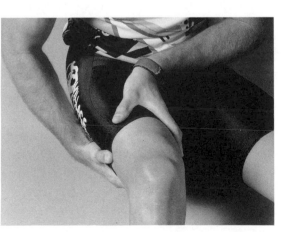

At the end of each section there is a quick-reference outline of the sequence you've just learned, without pictures. That way you can do the routine from the outline, once you've learned the techniques by name.

These are basic techniques that you can build on with other techniques you've learned or may learn in the future. You should take these techniques and combine them in the way that works best for you. Give it your personal touch, using these sequences as a guideline.

Where I've included self-massage techniques, I've put them first so you can practice on yourself before trying them on someone else. You'll learn what each stroke feels like and what kind of pressure it takes. Obviously, it's more relaxing to get a massage from someone else than to do it yourself.

Receiving a massage from another person takes some practice too. The first few times may be a bit uncomfortable. After all, you're in a vulnerable position, trusting another person with your body. A slight uneasiness is common for the first few massages. Soon you'll feel more comfortable and be able to relax and enjoy the massage.

Massage potions

Massage oil is used to decrease the friction between your hands and the area of the body you're working on. Put about a tablespoon in your palm and rub your hands together. This warms the oil before applying it to the body. Use just enough oil to lightly cover the area being massaged, but not so much that your hands slide uncontrollably.

I use Kool 'N Fit oil, which is formulated with a combination of light, pure ingredients (such as almond, avocado, grapeseed, safflower, sesame, and a vitamin E blend) that shouldn't clog pores or stain clothes.

Massage oil also can be used to protect skin in harsh weather and on cold, rainy rides, providing an extra layer between the skin and the elements to prevent dryness and windburn. On colder days, you can use a hot-feeling analgesic like Tiger Balm. Rub some around the knees to warm up before a ride.

On hot days, Kool 'N Fit Relieving Liquid is an alcohol-based product that leaves you feeling cool and invigorated. When I'm too tired to move after a ride, it feels great to spray it on my legs and put my feet up without rubbing it in. Or I spray it on my neck and shoulders on hot rides just to refresh.

A word about pressure

There are two levels of pressure mentioned in the routines that follow—medium and deep. Medium is a confident touch, firm but comfortable for the person receiving it. Deep is just shy of painful.

Deep strokes should be performed more slowly than medium-pressure strokes—otherwise they'll be painful to the athlete.

During a maintenance massage, an athlete may want a somewhat deeper stroke that at the time can be painful. That's okay, as long as the person receiving can distinguish "good" pain from "bad." After a good sports massage, some athletes experience soreness in the areas that were the tightest, where the massage therapist really "put the grind" to them. This pain should dissipate within a couple of days. These are troubled areas—after massage, they should be stretched.

Things to remember

• Be careful not to scratch the person you're massaging if you wear a watch or jewelry. For the same reason, keep your fingernails trimmed.

• When giving a massage to someone else, always position your body weight over the body part to which you are applying pressure. Let your weight do the work, not the muscles in your hands.

• Communication between the athlete and the massage-giver is critical. The massage should be deep but not to the point of discomfort for the athlete. Some pain is good, like the sensation you feel when pressure is applied between your shoulder blades. It hurts but you know it's a good pain that brings relief. You should always tell the person giving the massage if you are experiencing pain past your tolerance.

• The person receiving the massage should wear as little as they are comfortable with, but the massage-giver should keep the athlete warm by covering him or her with a towel, uncovering only the area being massaged.

• Do not apply pressure to superficial nerves and arteries, or to the popliteal space (behind the knee).

• Massage strokes almost always move toward the heart.

• Let your hands melt around the shape of the muscle you're working on. This is difficult to describe, but it's what's meant by acquiring a touch. It will come with experience.

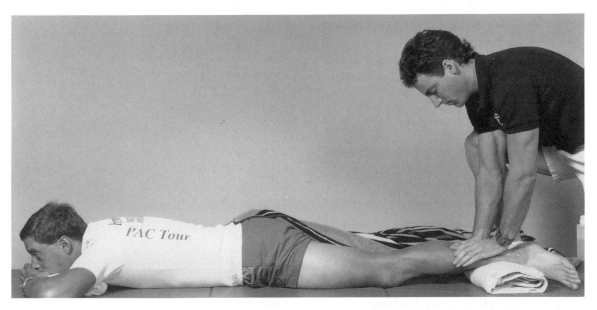

Position your body directly over the area you are working, using your body weight to apply pressure. This will make the massage less taxing for the giver.

Contraindications

Massage is not advisable in the presence of:

• Open wounds, road rash, burns, bruises, fever, or recent surgery. (You can work around road rash.)

• Infectious diseases of the skin, rashes, or athlete's foot.

• Fresh injuries that are still swollen or inflamed.

• Varicose veins or phlebitis.

• Bursitis.

• Second or third-degree sprain or strain.

• Cancerous growths.

• Any disease or condition that can be spread through the circulatory or lymphatic system. (Consult your physician.)

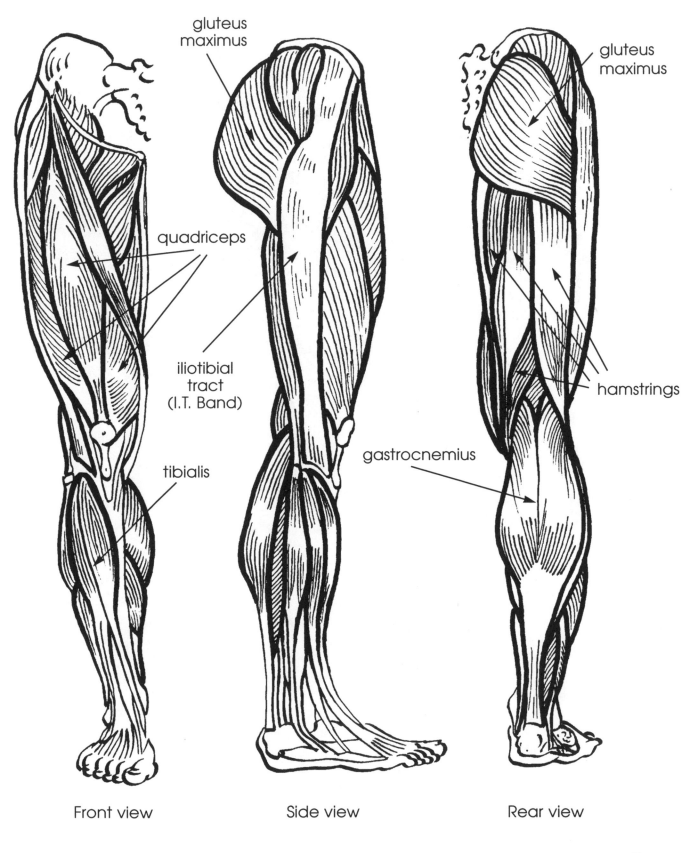

gluteus
maximus

gluteus
maximus

quadriceps

iliotibial
tract
(I.T. Band)

hamstrings

tibialis

gastrocnemius

Front view

Side view

Rear view

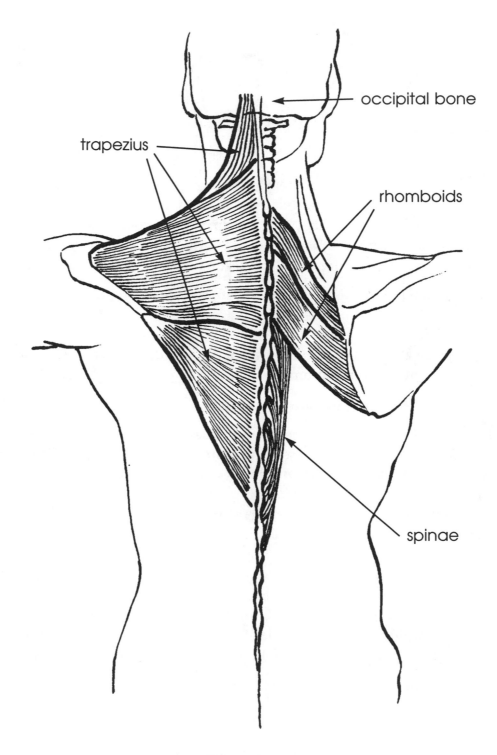

occipital bone

trapezius

rhomboids

spinae

Rear view

About pre-ride massage

Massage is a vital part of your preparation for a hard workout or competition. It gives you a jump start by warming the muscles, tendons, and ligaments. This "pre-heats" your body for the other parts of your pre-ride routine and prepares it to endure the demands to come. Massage makes the warm-up time on the bike more effective and can decrease the time needed to feel ready for hard efforts.

Here are some of the physical benefits of pre-ride massage.

- It improves circulation to tendons and ligaments.

- It helps break adhesions (muscle fibers that bundle up and need to be separated for improved freedom of movement).

- It leaves you with a warm, invigorated pair of legs.

The pre-ride or warm-up massage doesn't take the place of pre-ride stretching, but it will warm and relax the muscles so that the stretch is more effective. The massage should take place 20 to 30 minutes before your normal warm-up on the bike. (The on-bike warm-up should be about 10 to 15 minutes before an event.)

These techniques can also be done to revitalize your legs during breaks in a training ride or between events at a race. At those times, massage helps remove by-products of exercise and keeps legs from getting stiff or tight.

Pre-ride massage consists of compressions, crossfiber friction, and jostling. These are warming and invigorating techniques that are done without oil.

This work should be performed in a firm, repetitive manner, applying compressions to the belly, or middle, of the muscle and crossfiber friction to the tendons and ligaments. This routine should take about 10 minutes. Here's how to do the strokes.

Compressions: This stroke is performed with the palms of the hands compressing the muscle tissue in a rhythmic pumping motion, at a rate of about one per second and progressively deeper.

Crossfiber friction: These strokes are applied with the fingertips or thumb. Plant the fingertips on the skin, moving across the tendon in a sawing or circular motion. The fingers stay in the same place on the skin, while the skin slides across the muscle or tendon.

Direct pressure: This is applied with thumbs, fist, fingertips, or elbow to a sensitive spot in muscle or tendon. The area is stretched, stimulating fresh blood flow to relax and heal the troubled area. It should feel like a good hurt.

Jostling: Lay hands on the belly (middle) of the muscle and shake mildly to vigorously.

Percussion: A tapping, rhythmic movement, like drumming.

Pre-ride self-massage

Sit on the edge of a chair or on the floor against a back support. Each muscle group will take 30 to 60 seconds to massage. After doing the sequence a few times, you'll get a feel for the time needed for each.

These are the same techniques you'll use when giving a pre-ride massage to someone else. I've put the self-massage routine first, because you'll want to practice on yourself to learn what each technique feels like and what pressure it takes.

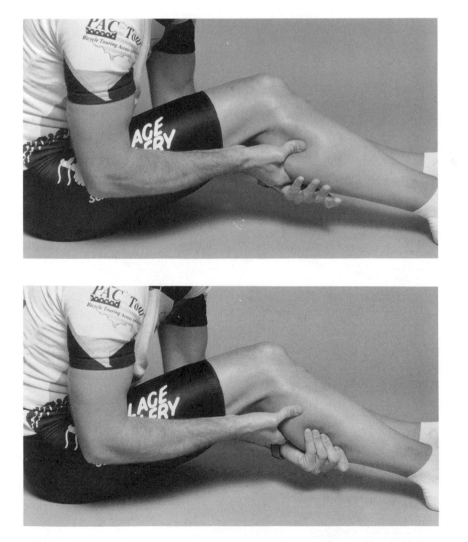

1. Grab and knead your calf, squeezing hands alternately.

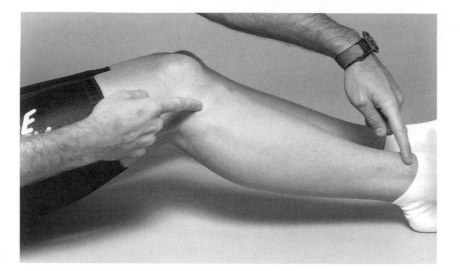

2. This next stroke will start near your ankle and be repeated, inching its way up to your knee.

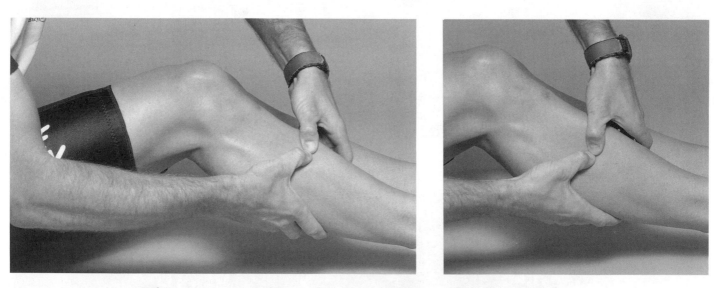

This is a crossfiber friction stroke. Using moderate pressure, saw across the muscles on the outside of your shin.

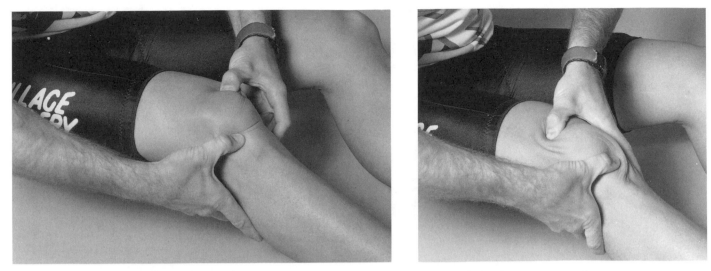

3. Do the same crossfiber move above and below your knee.

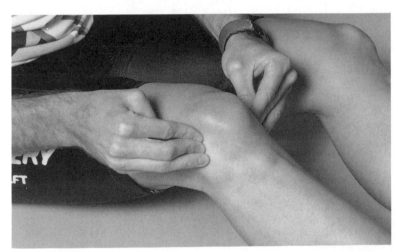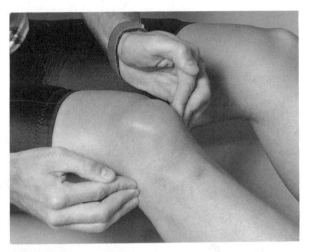

4. Moving in circles or up and down, apply pressure and friction to the ligaments that attach your upper and lower leg together.

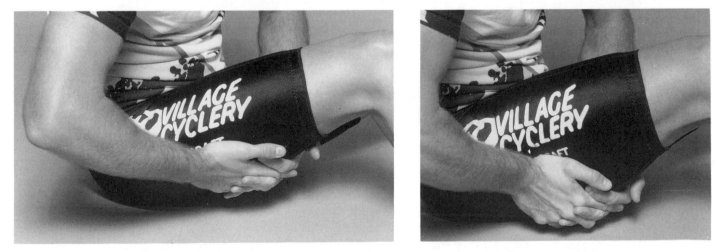

5. Moving the length of your hamstring muscle group toward your upper body, compress and release. Hamstrings are relaxed as compressions are applied.

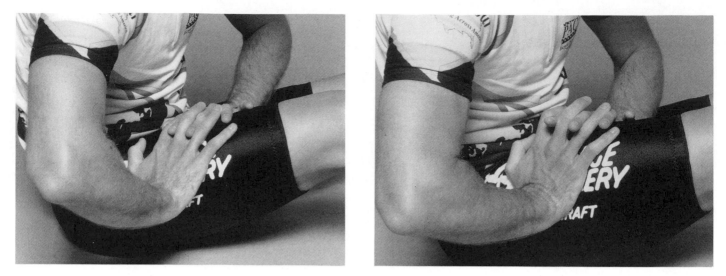

6. Compress and release your quadriceps muscle, moving from above your knee up the length of your thigh.

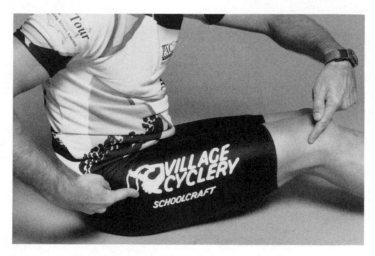

7. This next stroke will start outside your knee and go to the hip area.

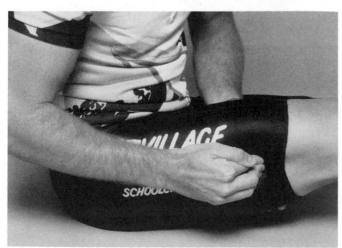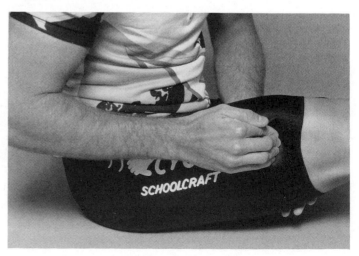

This is the same crossfiber friction move you did on your shin. Here you're working your iliotibial band, often tight in cyclists.

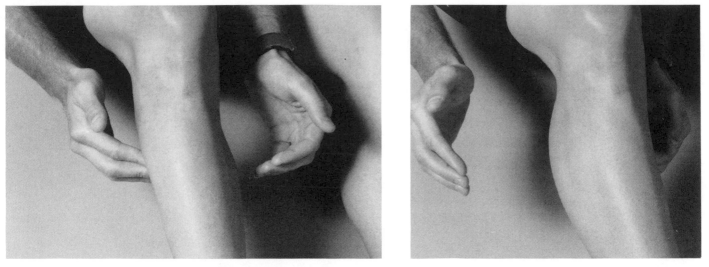

8. Percussion to your calf. Tap it back and forth.

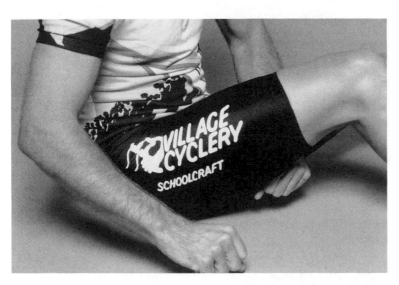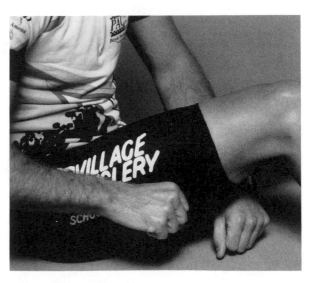

9. Percussion to your hamstrings

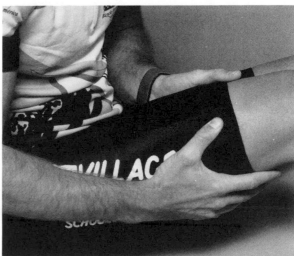

10. Jostle your thigh. Grab it and shake it from side to side.
Now repeat steps 1–10 on your other leg.

Pre-ride self-massage

❏ 1. Knead calf.

❏ 2. Crossfiber friction to outside of shin.

❏ 3. Crossfiber above and below knee.

❏ 4. Crossfiber to side of knee.

❏ 5. Compressions to hamstrings.

❏ 6. Compressions to quadriceps.

❏ 7. Crossfiber to iliotibial band
(outside of quad).

❏ 8. Tap calf side-to-side alternately.

❏ 9. Tap hamstrings with fists alternately.

❏ 10. Jostle thigh.

Do other leg.

Pre-ride massage

These techniques should be firm to be effective. Communication between the athlete and the person administering the massage should keep the pressure within the comfort zone. Keep your goal in mind – that you are manually warming the muscles and tendons.

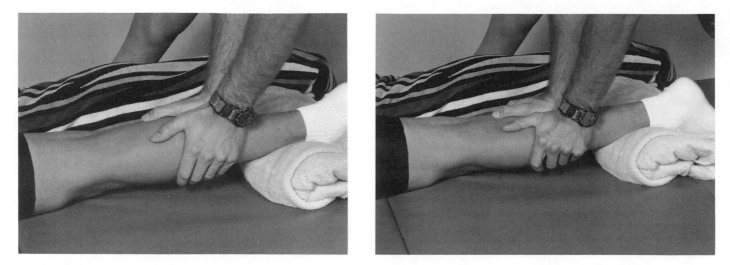

1. With the athlete face-down, apply compressions to the calves, straight down. A rolled-up towel may be put under the ankle for comfort. If in a cool place, keep the other leg covered.

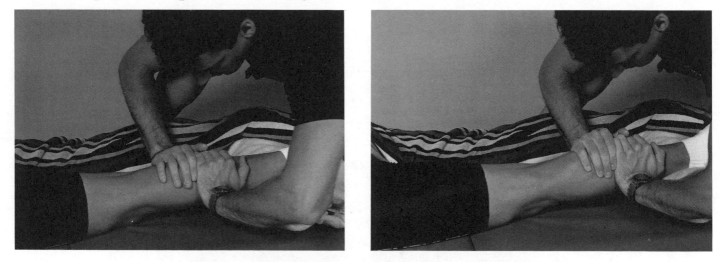

2. More calf compressions, pushing together.

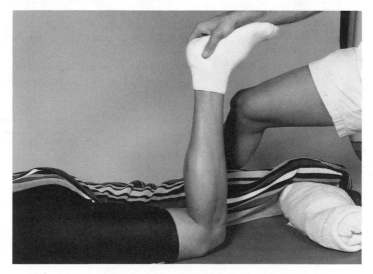

3. Grab the heel and swing the calf side to side.

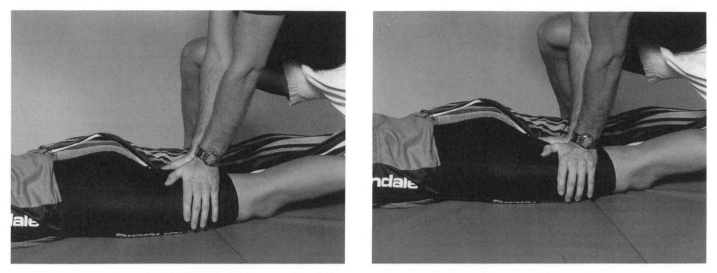

4. Compressions to the hamstrings, straight down.

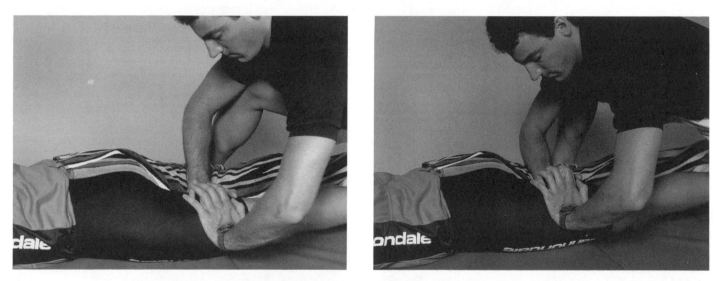

5. More hamstring compressions, pushing together.

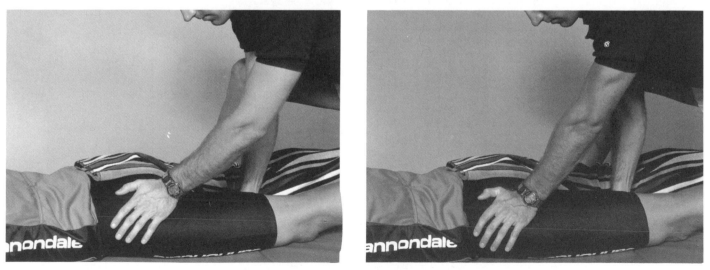

6. Compressions to the gluteals, with open hand.

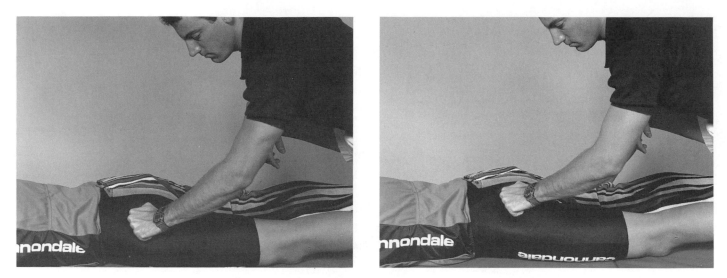

7. Direct pressure to the gluteals with the fist. (Direct pressure can also be applied with the elbow.) Shake glutes.

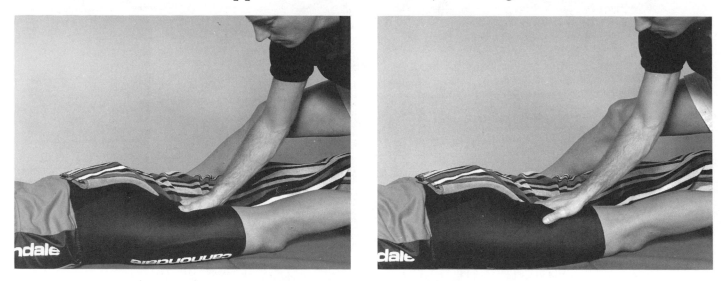

8. Jostling. Grab hamstrings and shake.
Repeat steps 1–8 on the athlete's other leg.

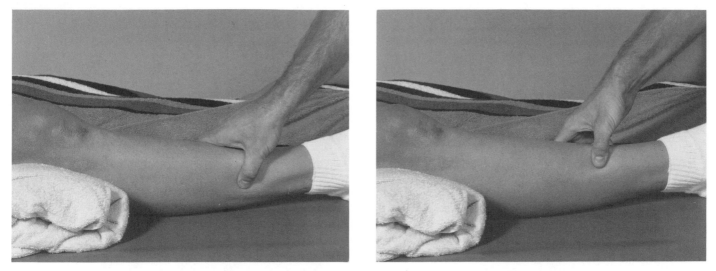

9. The athlete turns over and is now face up. Crossfiber friction stroke, the length of the shin. Towel may be placed under knee.

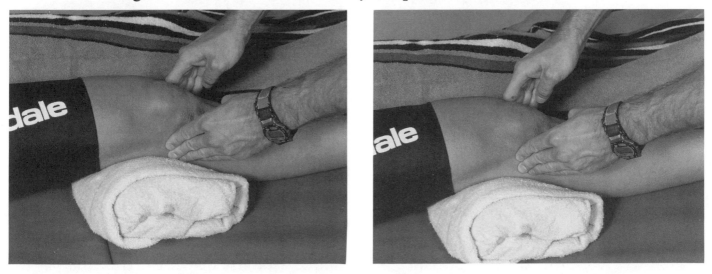

10. Crossfiber friction around the knee. Move in circles and up and down.

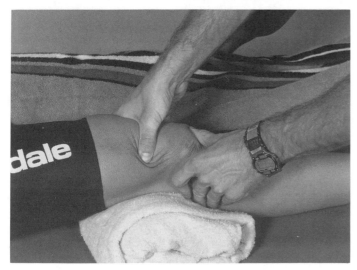
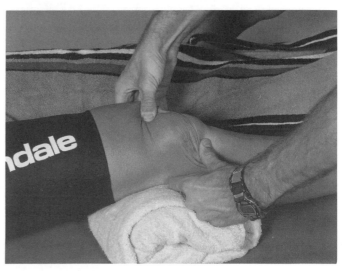

11. Crossfiber above and below the kneecap.

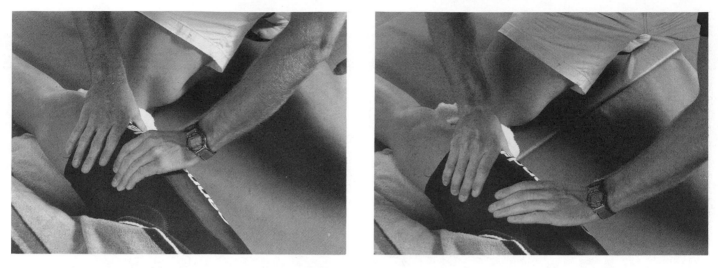

12. Knead the quadriceps, alternating the hand that squeezes. Move the length of the quad, beginning above the knee.

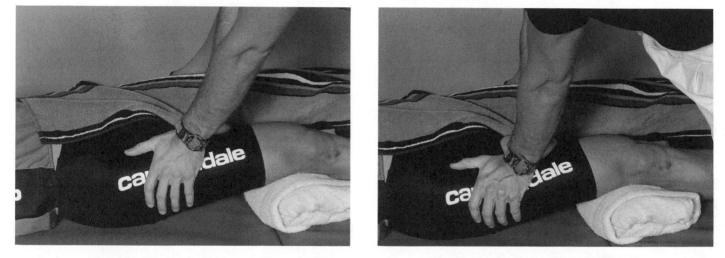

13. Compression, pressing both hands straight down on the quads. Be careful—this can be a sensitive area.

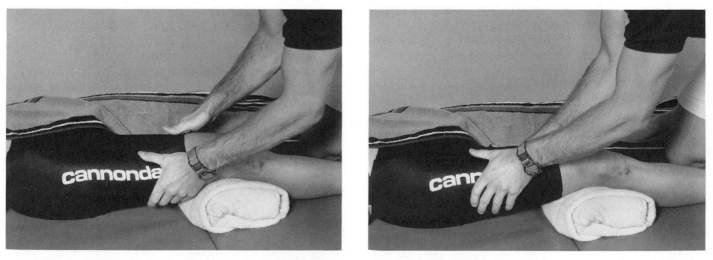

14. Jostle the quads. Grab the entire thigh and shake. Repeat steps 9–14 on the other leg.

Pre-ride massage

With athlete face-down:

❏ 1. Compressions to calf, straight down.

❏ 2. Compressions to calf, pushing together.

❏ 3. Grab heel and swing calf.

❏ 4. Compressions to hamstrings, straight down.

❏ 5. Compressions to hamstrings, pushing together.

❏ 6. Compressions to gluteals, with open hand.

❏ 7. Direct pressure to glutes with fist or elbow.

❏ 8. Jostle hamstrings and glutes.

Do other leg.

Turn athlete over, face-up:

❏ 9. Crossfiber friction to outside of shin.

❏ 10. Crossfiber to side of knee.

❏ 11. Crossfiber above and below knee.

❏ 12. Knead quadriceps.

❏ 13. Compressions to quads.

❏ 14. Jostle quads.

Do other leg.

About post-ride massage

Post-ride massage returns your muscles to a relaxed state after training or competition. Ideally, it should be done in a quiet, warm place after you've digested your meal. Just before bedtime is a good time.

This massage will flush your muscles of the waste products they produced during the ride and will stimulate fresh blood flow into the muscles. This will start the recovery process much sooner than if you hadn't intervened. That means you can get back into training sooner and harder.

These techniques will also help prevent the delayed onset of soreness, undue fatigue, and insomnia. They should leave you with a calm feeling, possibly drowsy.

There are four basic techniques for this post-ride massage: effleurage, strips, spreading, and hacking. Oil is required. Apply medium pressure, but always be in the comfort zone. Muscles are likely to be tender in a post-ride massage, so if you're massaging someone else, talk to him or her and ask if the pressure is okay.

Here's how to do the strokes.

Effleurage or flushing: This stroke is done with an open hand, and pressure is applied with the entire hand. Let your hand melt around and mold to the shape of the muscle you are working. Always move the strokes toward the heart.

Effleurage assists your body's natural process of pushing the waste products of exercise through the body's filtering system, thus speeding your recovery dramatically.

Strips: These are done with your thumbs forming an upside-down V. It's a deep stroke, so move slowly or it will hurt. Move your thumbs toward the heart up the length of the muscle (in strips). Communicate to stay within the athlete's comfort zone.

Spreading: The hands start together, pushing down and then spreading apart, which spreads and separates the muscle.

Hacking: The finishing touch that I like to use is called hacking. It's the karate-chop motion you see masseurs using in old movies. It's a percussion move that leaves the muscles feeling tingly and invigorated.

Here's how it's done. Start with open hands, fingers spread apart. With each percussion, let your relaxed fingers smack together. Get into a rhythm, moving up and down the legs.

As in the pre-ride section. I've put the self-massage routine first so you can practice the techniques on yourself before trying them on someone else.

Post-ride self-massage

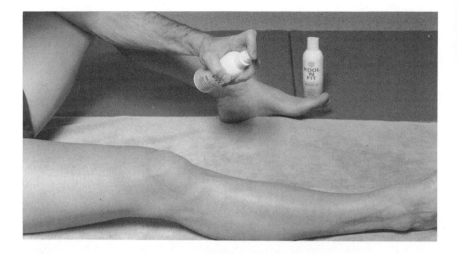

1. Spray on Kool 'N Fit or other pain reliever, if desired. Applied to your legs beforehand, the spray helps thin the oil. Or you can pour a half ounce or so of the pain reliever into the oil bottle.

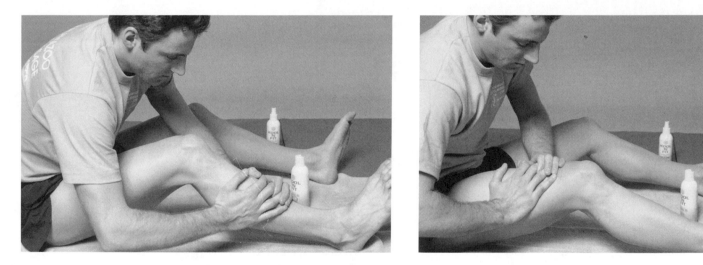

Apply oil. Spread over your entire leg.

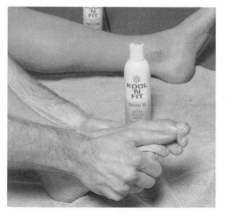 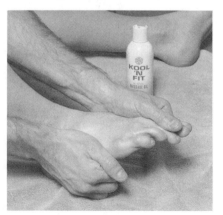 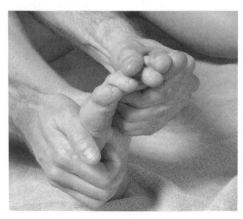

2. Grab your foot and spread your hands outward.
Dig your fingertips into the sole of the foot, moving from heel to toes.

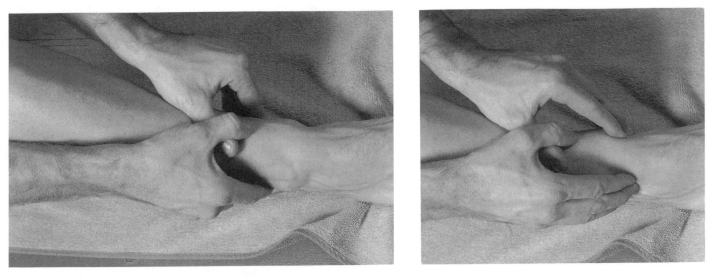

3. Move your fingertips around your ankle bone in small circles.

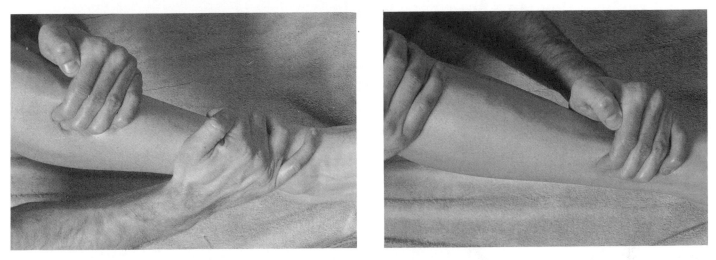

4. Dig the fingertips of one hand and the palm of the other into the muscle outside of your shin. Alternate pulling from ankle to knee.

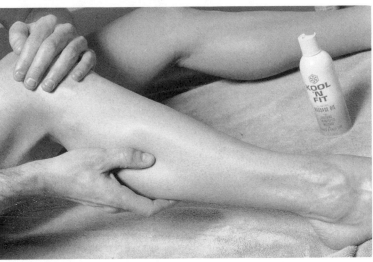

5. Crossfiber friction stroke with your thumb from the outside of your shin to the inside of your calf. Inch your way down from ankle to knee.

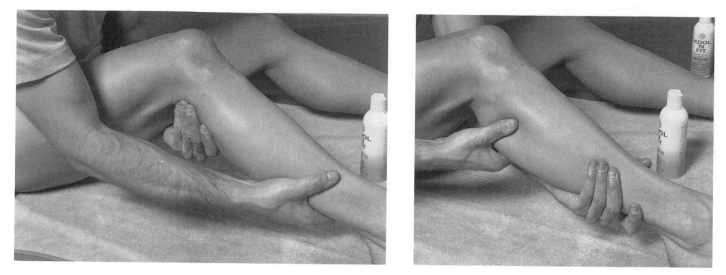

6. Flushing stroke. Alternating hands, pull from your ankle to your knee with firm pressure.

7. Position your hand with fingertips together like this.

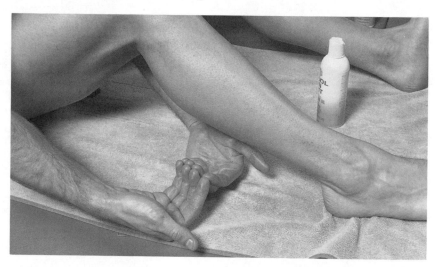

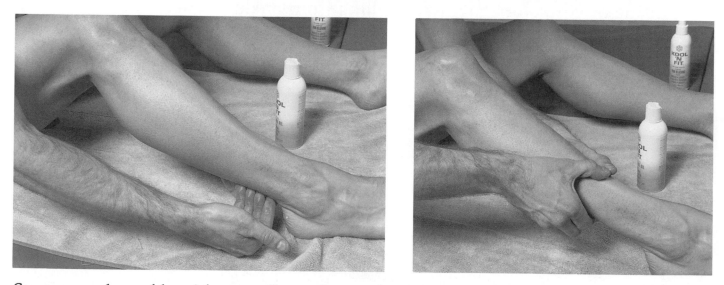

Start near the ankle with your fingertips and stroke the entire calf. Start on the outside and make strips up the calf, working your way to the other side of the calf.

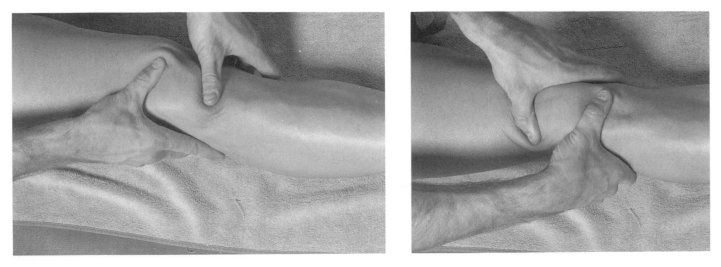

8. Move your thumbs back and forth around your kneecap.

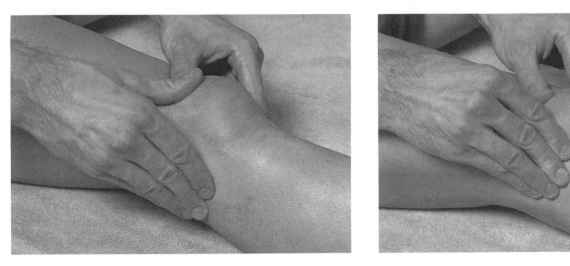

9. Using an up-and-down and a circular motion alternately, work your fingertips (not your thumbs) on the inside and outside of your knee.

10. Flushing stroke to your hamstrings, pulling towards you from knee to hip with alternate hands.

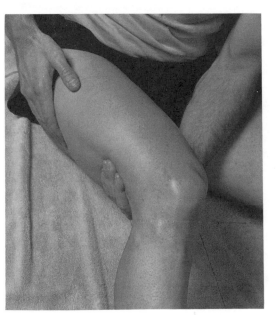
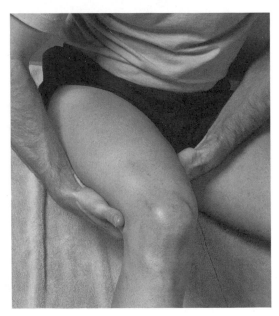

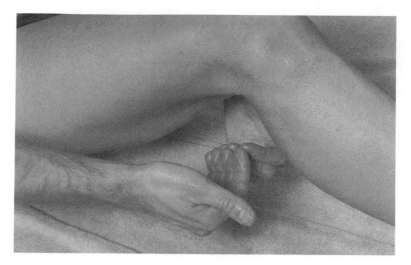

11. Put your fingertips together like this.

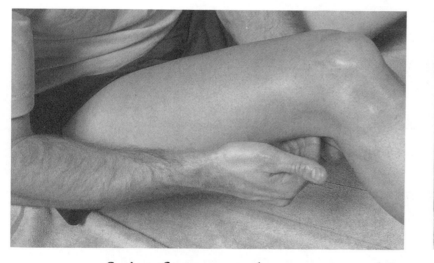

Strips from your knee to your hip, working from the outside of your leg to the inside.

12. Spreading stroke. Start with your hands together and push down and apart. Work the entire length of your quadriceps.

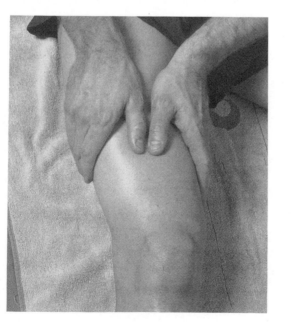

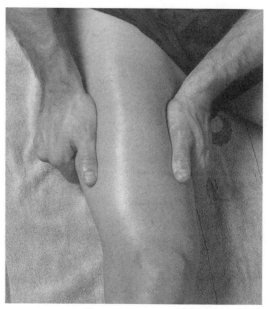

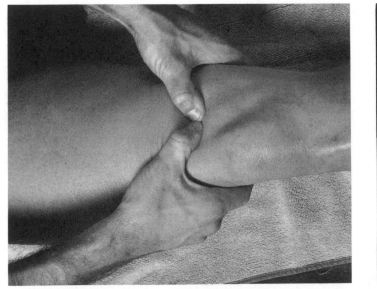 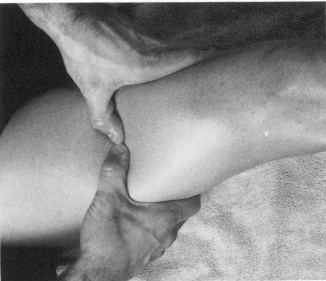

13. Deep strips to your quads with your thumbs, pulling towards you from your knee to the top of your thigh.

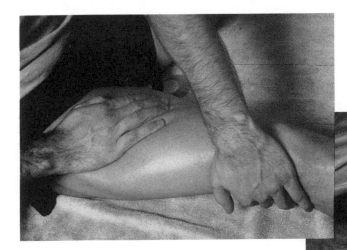

14. Final flushing stroke, alternating hands pulling across your quads.

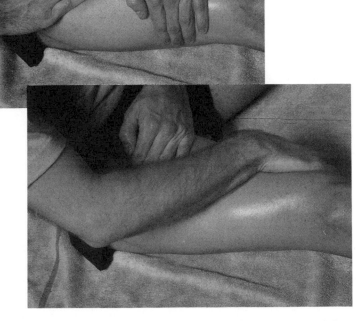

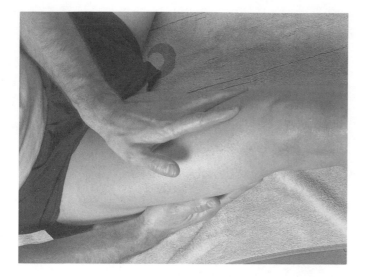 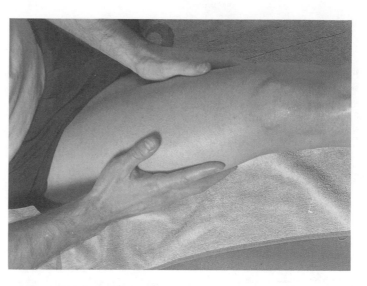

15. Repeat all the steps on your other leg.
Finish up with some jostling.
Grab and shake.

Post-ride self-massage

- ❏ 1. Apply oil over entire leg.
- ❏ 2. Spread foot. Press sole with fingertips.
- ❏ 3. Circles around ankle.
- ❏ 4. Deep strips outside of shin, pulling to the knee.
- ❏ 5. Crossfiber outside of shin, pulling to the knee.
- ❏ 6. Flush calf.
- ❏ 7. Strips to calf with thumbs.
- ❏ 8. Half circle around kneecap.
- ❏ 9. Circles to side of knee.
- ❏ 10. Flush hamstrings, alternating hands.
- ❏ 11. Strips with thumbs to hamstrings.
- ❏ 12. Spreading stroke to quads, pushing down and apart.
- ❏ 13. Strips to quads.
- ❏ 14. Flush quads, alternating hands.
- ❏ 15. Jostling.
- ❏ 16. Hacking.

Do other leg.

Post-ride massage

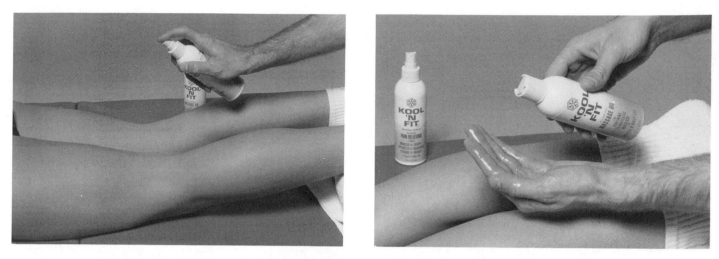

1. Spray on Kool 'N Fit, if desired. Apply oil and spread it over the entire back of the leg with firm pressure.

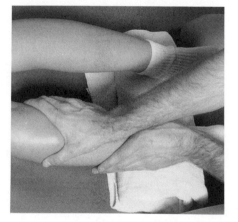 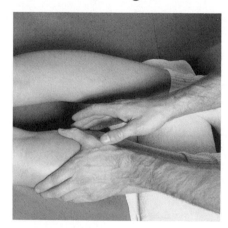 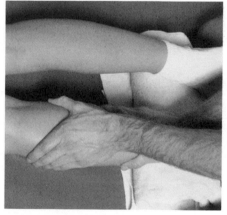

2. Flush the calf, with alternating hands pushing toward the athlete's heart. Firm pressure.

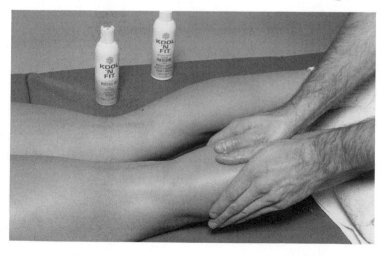 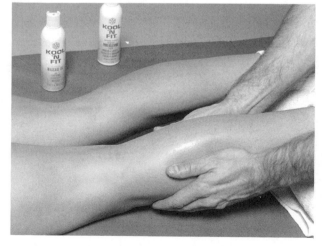

3. Spread the calf muscles. With open hands, press down and separate.

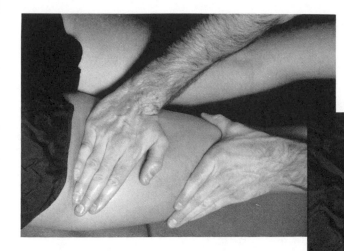

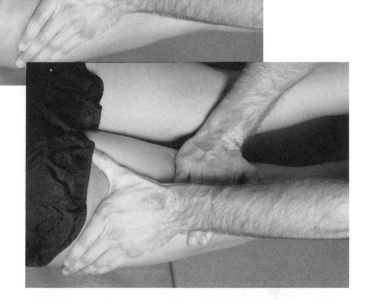

4. Flush the hamstrings upward toward the heart with alternating hands. Firm pressure.

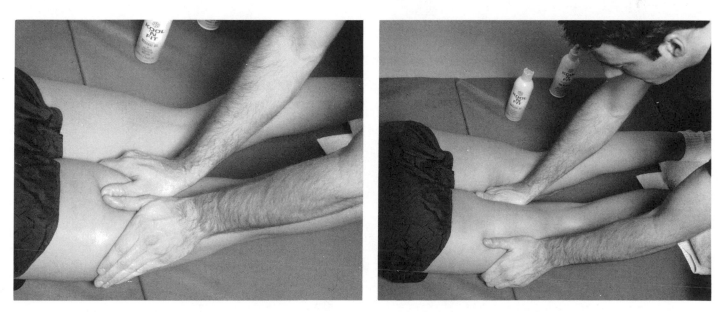

5. Spread the hamstrings, starting with hands together then separating.

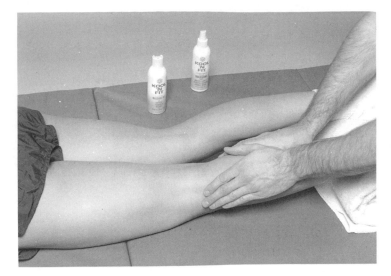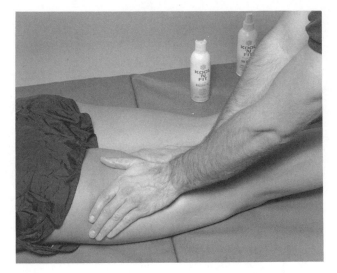

6. Flush the entire leg. Do steps 1-6 on the other leg.

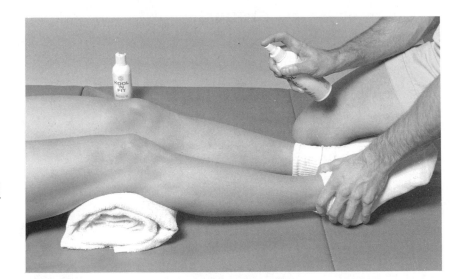

7. The athlete turns over and is now face up. Spray Kool 'N Fit on the front of the legs, if desired.

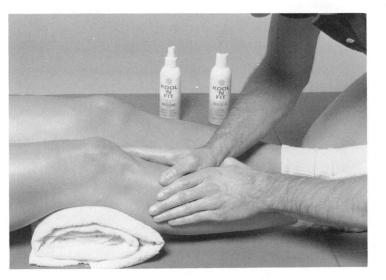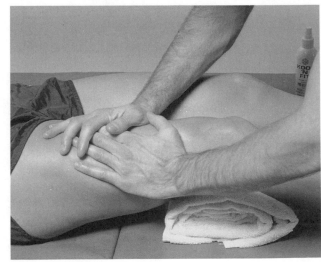

Spread oil over the entire leg.

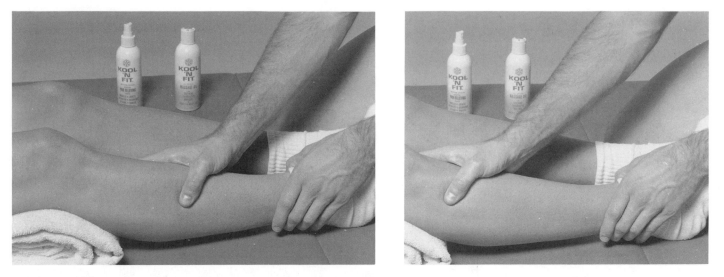

8. Working the outside of the leg from the ankle to the knee, alternately push the thumb from one hand and palm from the other upward. Repeat.

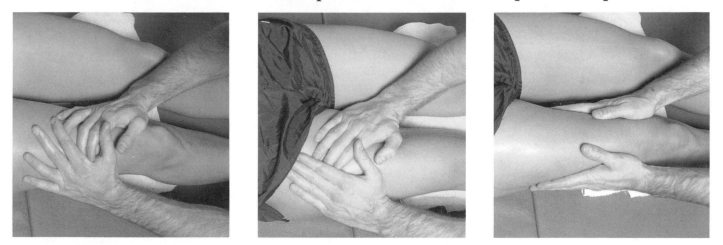

9. Flush the quadriceps upward (toward the heart) with firm pressure (left and center photos). Use light pressure to glide back to the starting position above the knee (right photo).

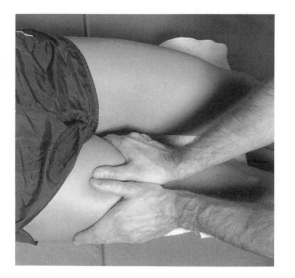

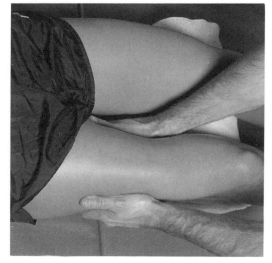

10. Spread the quads, starting with hands together then separate.

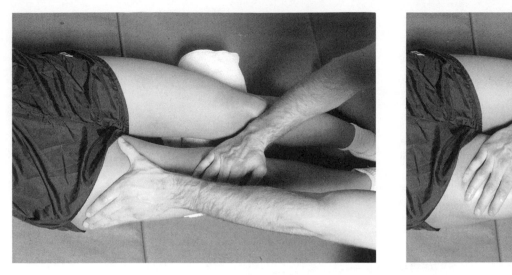

11. Flush the quads, alternating hands.
    Then flush the entire leg.
    Finish up with some jostling or hacking.
    Repeat steps 7-11 on the other leg.

Post-ride massage

With athlete face-down:

❏ 1. Apply oil to back of legs.

❏ 2. Flush calf, alternating hands.

❏ 3. Spread calf, pushing down and separating.

❏ 4. Flush hamstrings, alternating hands.

❏ 5. Spread hamstrings, pushing down and separating.

❏ 6. Flush entire leg.

Do other leg.

Turn athlete over, face-up:

❏ 7. Apply oil to front of legs.

❏ 8. Stroke outside of shin, alternating hands, thumb, and palm.

❏ 9. Flush quadriceps.

❏ 10. Spread quads.

❏ 11. Flush quads, alternating hands.

❏ 12. Flush entire leg.

❏ 13. Hacking.

Do other leg.

Maintenance massage

Maintenance massage is the massage you'll use most often because it helps keep you tuned up for the big race or tour. Done regularly, it will put you in touch (excuse the pun) with your body. You'll feel aches and pains you didn't know you had. That's good because you'll be able to work on these troubled areas before they become a problem.

This massage will help maintain proper muscle, fiber, tendon, and ligament function by speeding post-ride recovery. You'll be able to rest more comfortably and train sooner with less discomfort due to fatigue.

By keeping your muscles, tendons, and ligaments more pliable and spasm-free through regular massage, you'll be less susceptible to injury, more flexible, and stronger as a whole. It's through massage, smart training (including weight training), and stretching that you'll recover and train most effectively.

Basically, maintenance massage is a post-ride massage (adding some crossfiber strokes for their corrective effect), but the pressure applied is much firmer.

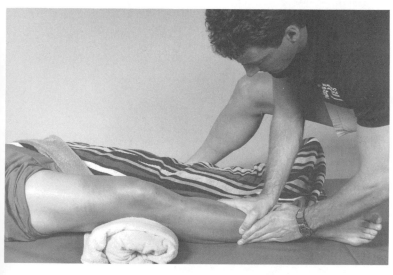

1. Spread oil over the entire leg. (Towel under knee is optional.)

Carefully go around the kneecap.

Communicate with the athlete. Is the pressure of the stroke too light? too deep? Find out.

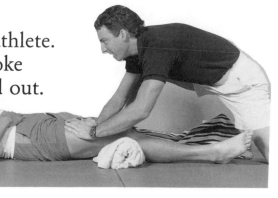

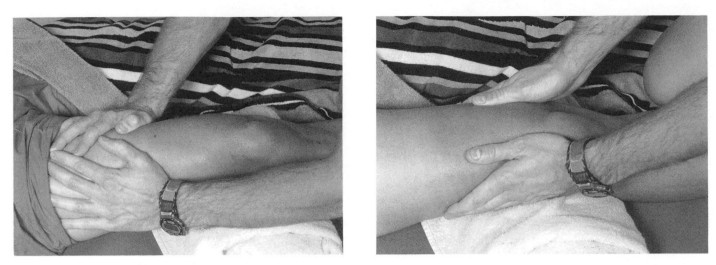

2. Two-handed flushing stroke starting above the knee and moving upward with firm pressure (photo at left).
   Glide back to the starting point with light pressure (photo at right).

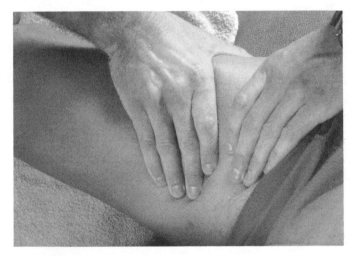 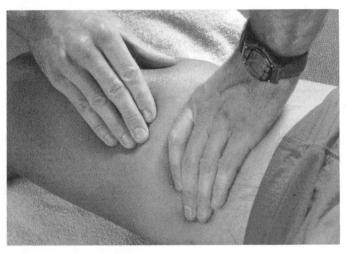

3. Knead the quadriceps with firm pressure. Get into a back-and-forth rhythm, with alternating hands grabbing the quads.

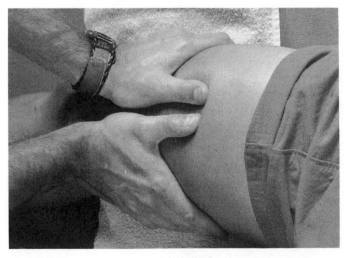 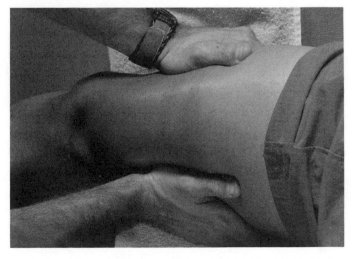

4. Spreading stroke to the quads, starting with your hands together, then separating.

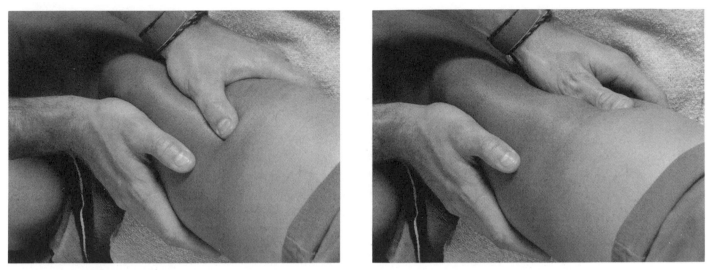

5. Crossfiber spreading stroke with your thumbs. Start in the center of the quad, stroking outward. Work the entire length of the quad on the outside, then work the inside half.

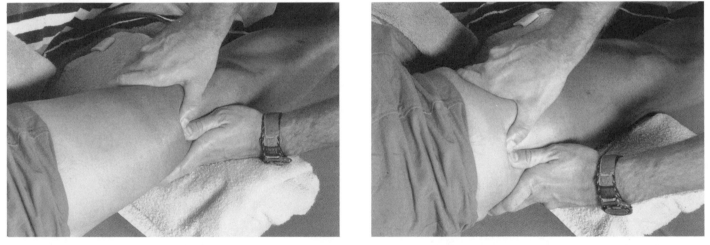

6. Deep strips, starting above the knee and going to the top of the thigh. Then move over a thumb width for the next strip.

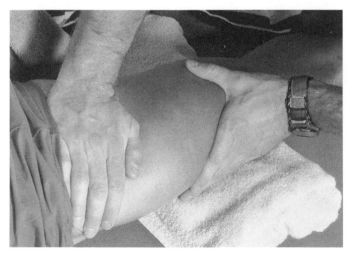
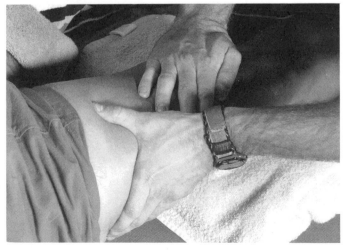

7. Flush the quads, alternating hands.

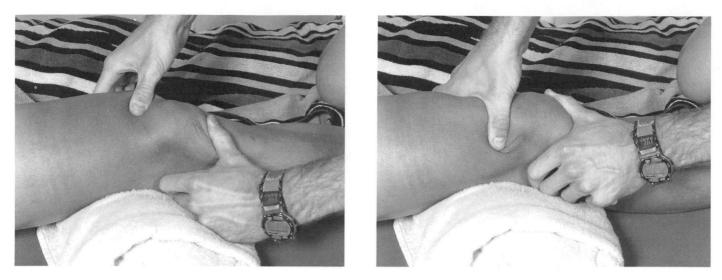

8. Crossfiber friction above and below the knee.

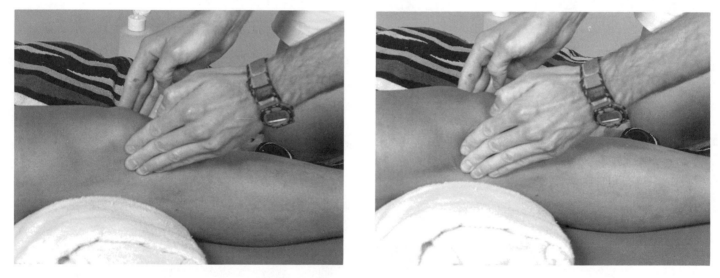

9. Crossfiber friction to the sides of the knee, both up and down and in circles.

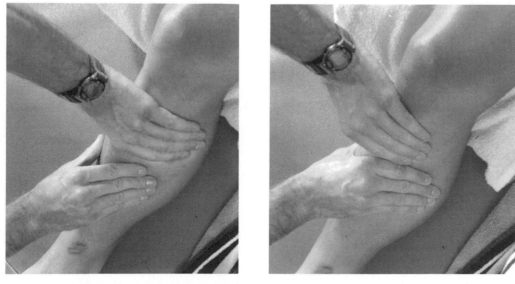

10. Knead the lower leg muscle on the outside of the shin with your thumbs.

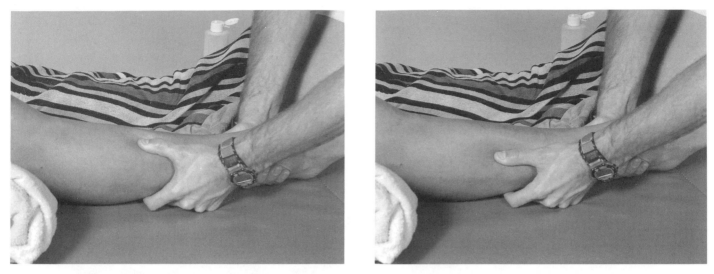

11. Crossfiber stroke to the outside of the shin. It feels like twanging guitar strings. This area may be tender, so communicate with the athlete.

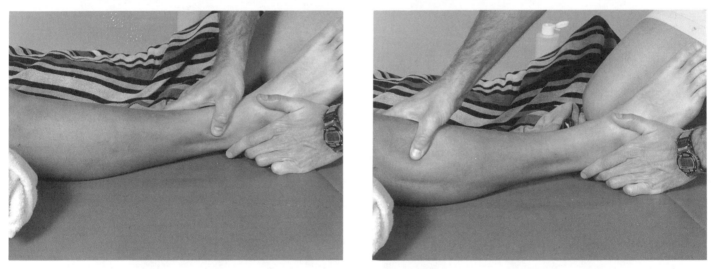

12. Deep strips with your thumb up the outside of the shin.

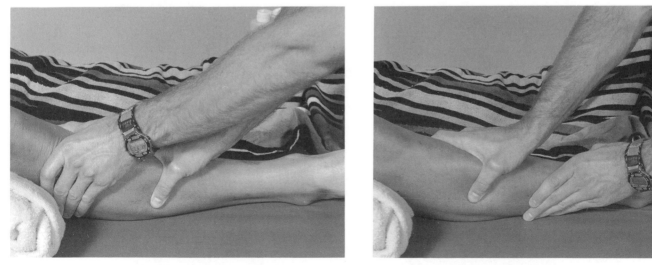

13. Alternate hands, flushing the muscles on the outside of the shin.

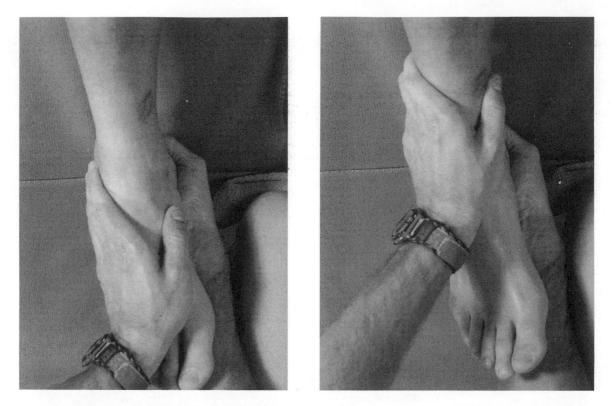

14. Holding the heel in one hand for support, stroke the top of the foot firmly upward to the ankle.

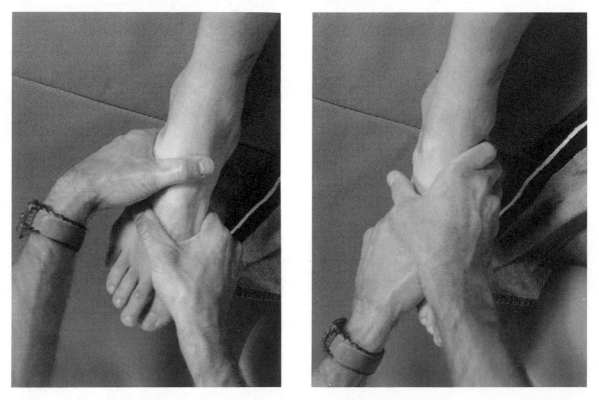

15. Grab the foot and pull or wring it with alternating hands. Then flush the entire leg as one stroke, just like at the beginning when you applied oil. Repeat steps 1-15 on the other leg.

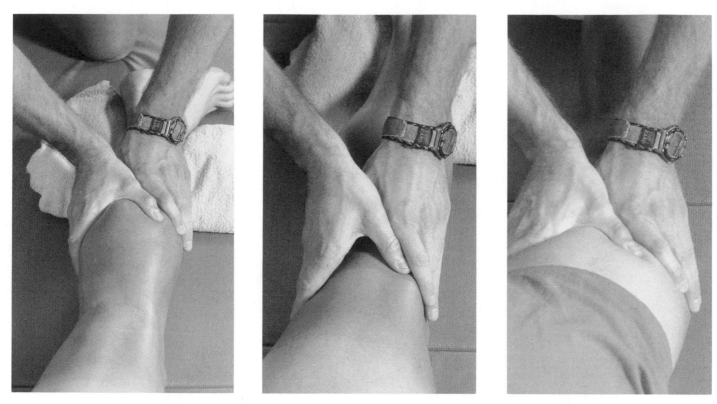

16. The athlete now turns over. Spread oil on the back of the leg. Do not use pressure over the back of the knee.

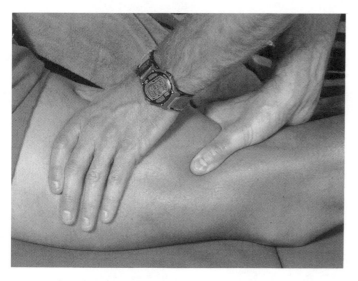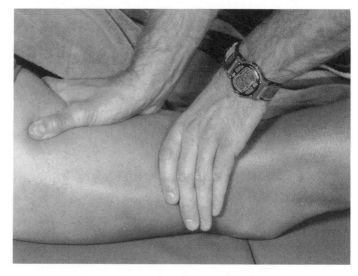

17. Flushing stroke to the hamstrings, with alternate hands.

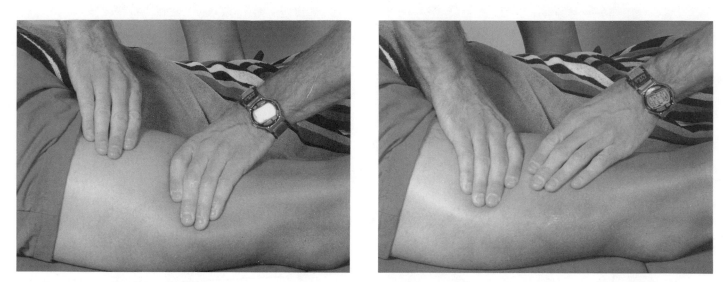

18. Knead the hamstrings, grabbing and squeezing with alternating hands.

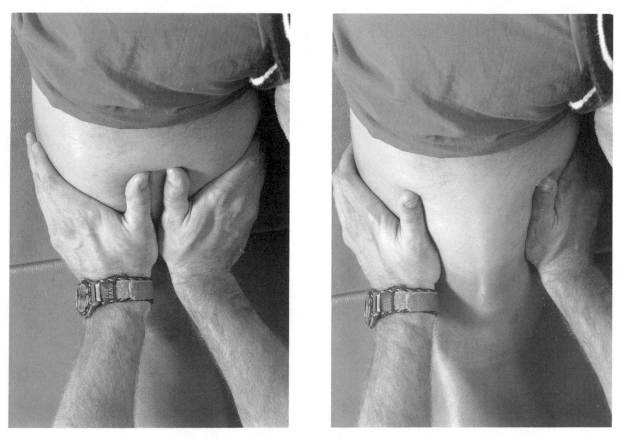

19. Spreading stroke to the hamstrings with open hands.
Press your hands down and apart with firm pressure.

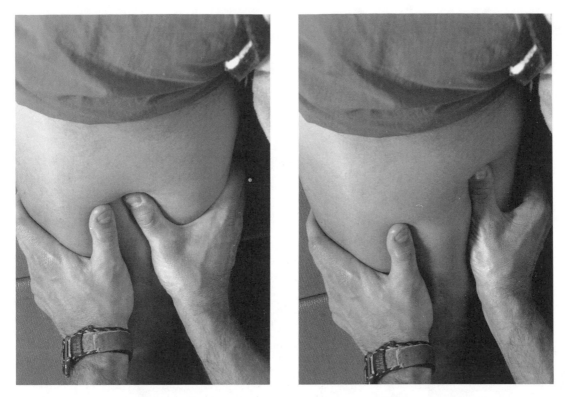

20. Crossfiber spreading stroke. Start with your thumbs in the center, moving one inward. Work down the entire hamstring, then repeat on the outside with the other thumb. Use firm pressure.

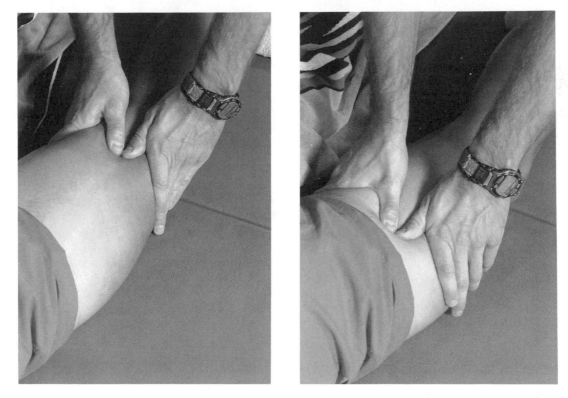

21. Deep strips to the hamstrings. Start above the knee and press your thumbs in a strip up the hamstring (toward the heart). Glide your hands lightly back to the knee. It will take about 8 to 10 strips to cover the entire width of the hamstring.

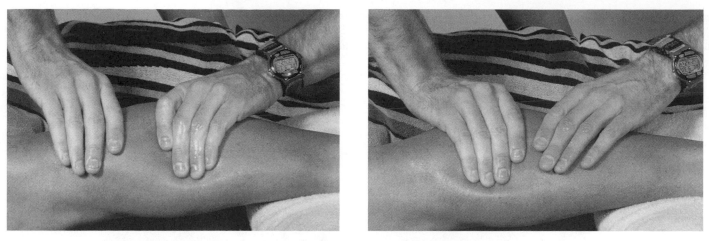

23. Knead the calf rhythmically, grabbing and squeezing with alternating hands.

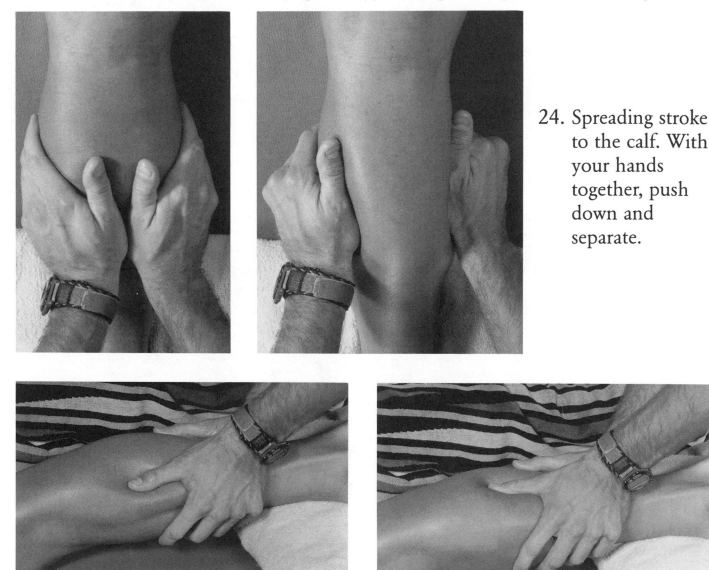

24. Spreading stroke to the calf. With your hands together, push down and separate.

25. Crossfiber stroke to the calf. Hands together, using your thumb, start at the center of the calf and stroke toward the outside. Work the entire outside length of the calf with one thumb, then repeat with the other thumb on the inside.

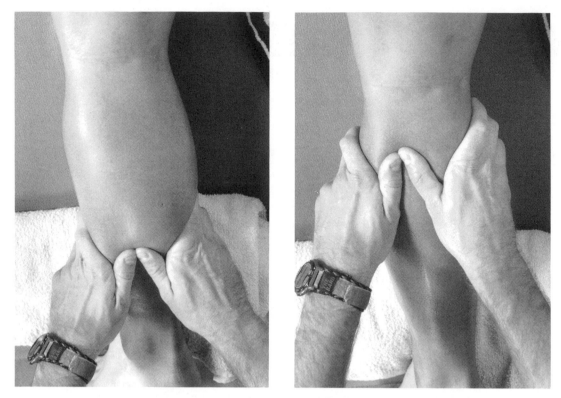

26. Deep strips to the calf. Move slowly and work the entire calf. This area is usually tender, so start lightly and increase the pressure as the athlete requests it.

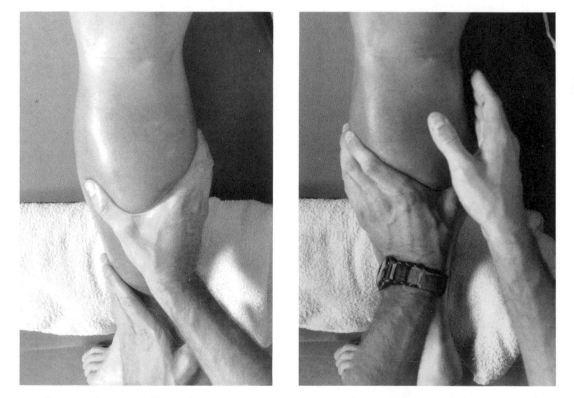

27. Flush the calf with firm pressure. Then flush the entire leg. Finish with some jostling and hacking. Repeat steps 16-27 on the other leg.

QUICK REFERENCE:

Maintenance massage

- ❏ 1. Spread oil over entire leg, with athlete face up.
- ❏ 2. Flush quadriceps, two-handed.
- ❏ 3. Knead quads.
- ❏ 4. Spread quads with open hands.
- ❏ 5. Crossfiber to quads, outer then inner, with thumbs.
- ❏ 6. Deep strips to quads.
- ❏ 7. Flush quads, alternating hands.
- ❏ 8. Crossfiber stroke above and below knee.
- ❏ 9. Crossfiber stroke to side of knee.
- ❏ 10. Knead muscle outside of shin, with thumbs.
- ❏ 11. Crossfiber to outside of shin.
- ❏ 12. Strips up outside of shin, with thumbs.
- ❏ 13. Flush outer shin.

❑ 14. Stroke top of foot.

❑ 15. Wring foot with pulling stroke. Flush entire leg.

Do steps 1-15 on other leg.

❑ 16. Turn over. Apply oil to back of leg.

❑ 17. Flushing stroke to hamstrings.

❑ 18. Knead hamstrings.

❑ 19. Spread hamstrings with open hands.

❑ 20. Crossfiber with thumbs to hamstrings.

❑ 21. Deep strips to hamstrings.

❑ 22. Flush hamstrings again.

❑ 23. Knead calf.

❑ 24. Spread calf with open hands.

❑ 25. Crossfiber to calf with thumbs

❑ 26. Strips to calf.

❑ 27. Flush calf with alternating hands.

❑ 28. Flush entire leg.

❑ 29. Hacking and/or jostling.

Do steps 16–29 on other leg

Neck and shoulder massage

This neck and shoulder sequence is a quick and effective way to relieve the tightness in your upper back between your shoulder blades (rhomboids) and the muscle that makes your shoulders shrug toward your ears (trapezius). This is a very common area for tension. Whether it's caused by mental or physical stress, it leaves you hunching over the handlebars of your bike or the computer at work. It is often a burning or dull ache between your shoulder blades.

Oh yes, this is also the routine you'll use when friends (or strangers) at a party find out that you know some massage techniques. They'll come up to you and drop hints, or just point at their shoulders.

This five-minute routine is done without oil and is great any time — whenever you feel that annoying tightness trying to creep up your neck. Best of all, of course, is to do it before tension starts to take its toll.

In this and the following routine you can do each side as you go along or do everything on one side and go back and repeat on the other side.

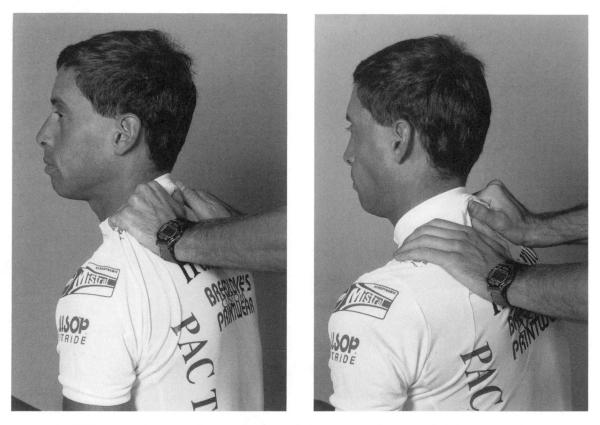

1. Warm the neck and shoulder area by grabbing and squeezing the trapezius, alternating hands.

53

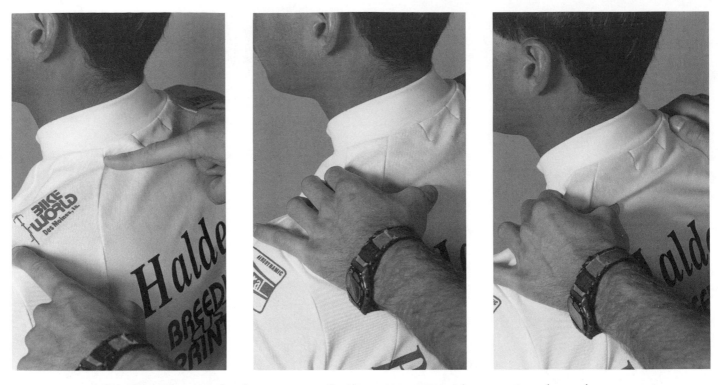

2. This move works between the two points shown in the photo at left. With your thumb and first finger pinch the trapezius and inch your way across. This will be very sensitive for some, so work inside their tolerance. I also refer to this as the "Spock" (Star Trek) move. It should be a good hurt (meaning sensitive, yet pain-relieving).

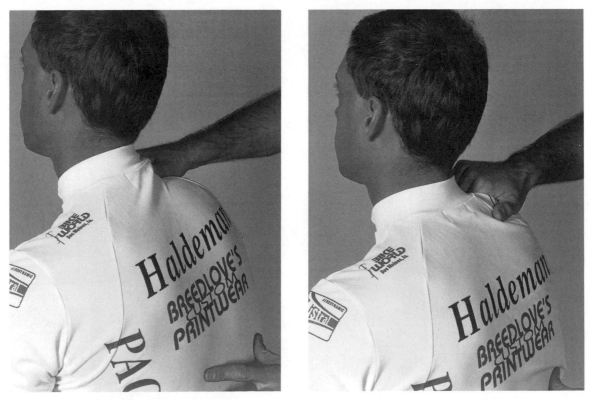

3. Grab the trapezius and shake out the area just worked. Make it feel good.

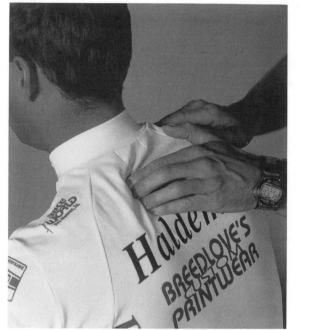 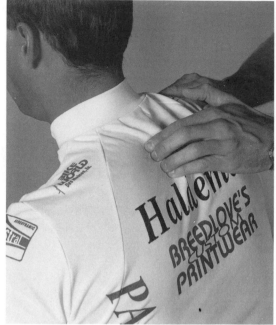

4. Moving from left to right, apply friction between the spine and the shoulder blade. You'll feel the muscles that run along the spine. Move across them.
Work all the way down the spine if you want.
Repeat on the other side.

5. Apply direct pressure with your thumb to the rhomboids, the area between the shoulder blade and spine. Inch your way down. Press on each spot for 5-30 seconds, slowly increasing pressure. (You could begin with 5 seconds and work your way up to 30.) This is a good hurt.

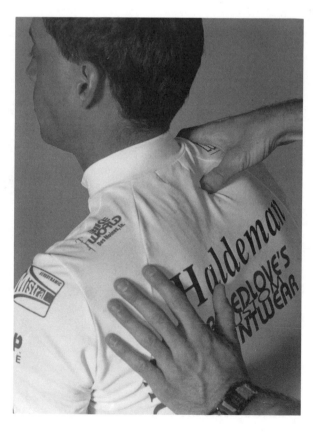

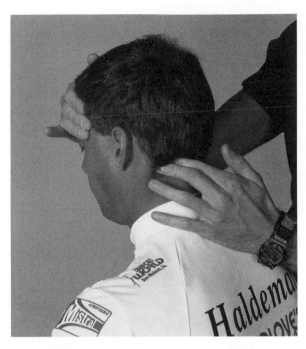

6. Dig just below the occipital bone area, that little bump on the back of the skull. Crossfiber with good pressure.

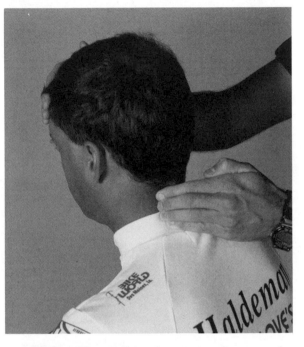

7. Crossfiber friction to the neck. Dig in. Work back and forth.

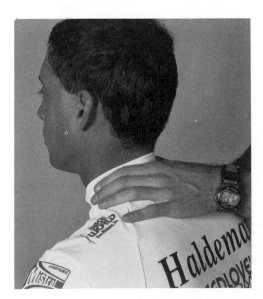

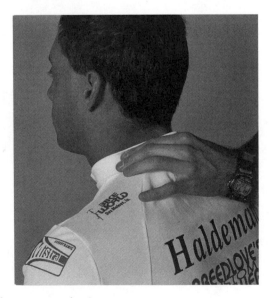

8. Squeeze neck several times.

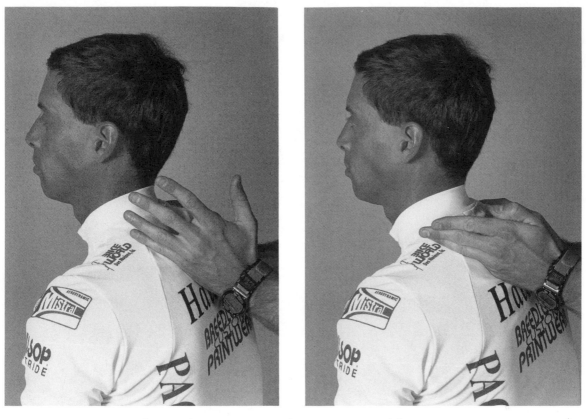

9. Hacking is a percussion move. Alternate your hands, getting into a rhythm, going over all the areas just worked.

Neck and shoulder massage

❑ 1. Grab traps and squeeze alternately.

❑ 2. Pinch traps with the "Spock Grip."

❑ 3. Shake traps.

❑ 4. Crossfiber between spine and shoulder blade.

❑ 5. Direct pressure between spine and shoulder blade.

❑ 6. Crossfiber to occipital bone.

❑ 7. Crossfiber to neck.

❑ 8. Grab and squeeze neck with one hand.

❑ 9. Hacking. (Karate chop.)

Neck massage

Here is another neck massage routine. Oil and different techniques are used in this one. This is more neck-specific than the neck and shoulder routine described on the previous pages. These techniques are more soothing – great after a ride, before bed.

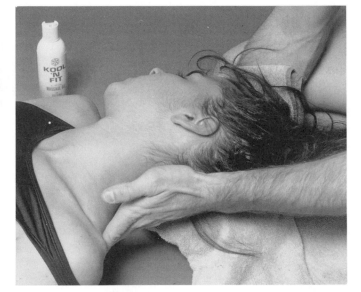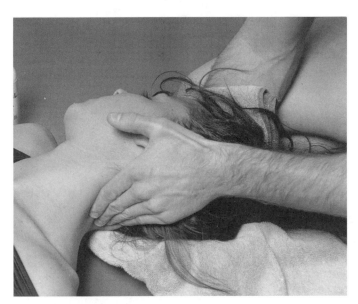

1. Hold the head in your right hand, with a towel between your hand and the athlete's hair. Apply oil with your open left hand, moving from the shoulder to the base of the skull (hairline).

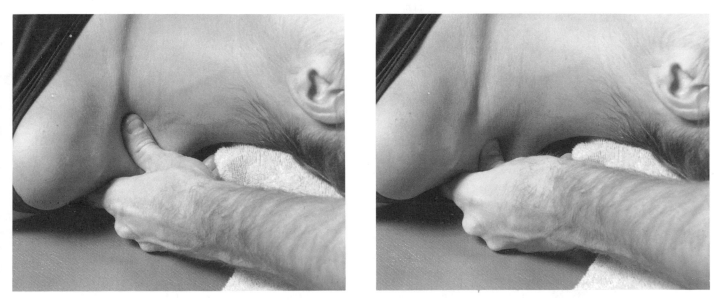

2. Move your thumb across the trapezius muscle with a crossfiber stroke.

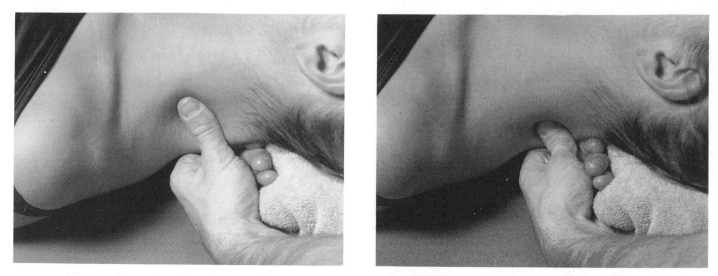

3. The same crossfiber stroke, inching your way up the neck.

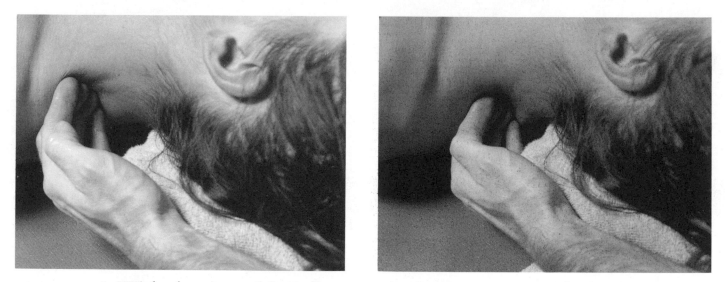

4. With the tips of four fingers, zigzag your way up the neck.

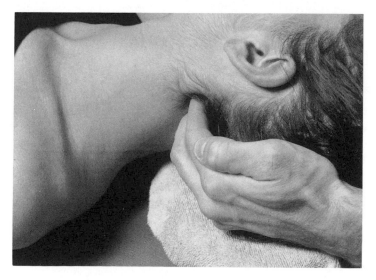

5. Dig your fingers below the occipital bone area, that bump in the back of the skull. Apply direct pressure just below the occipital bone.
Hold 5-30 seconds.

Repeat all on other side.

Caution: If the athlete has neck pain or previous neck injuries, omit steps 6 and 7.

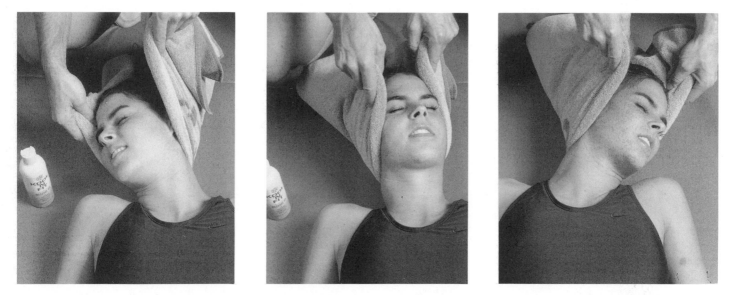

6. Cradle the head in the towel and slowly swing it from side to side.

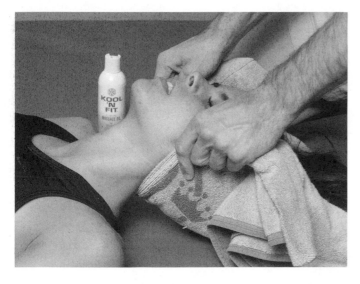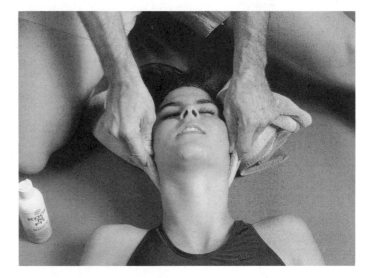

7. Light traction can be applied with the towel. Gently pull up and straight back.

Neck massage

❏ 1. Apply oil from shoulder to hairline.

❏ 2. Crossfiber to traps.

❏ 3. Crossfiber to neck.

❏ 4. Four-finger stroke, shoulder to neck.

❏ 5. Direct pressure to occipital bone area.

Repeat 1-5 on other side.

(Omit 6 and 7 if any neck problems.)

❏ 6. Cradle head in towel. Swing.

❏ 7. Traction. Pull up and straight back.

Lower back massage

This routine emphasizes loosening the lower back and buttock area (gluteals). These two muscle groups are so closely related that both must be relaxed for either to be. Usually when your back is tight, your gluteals are already tight and have started pulling on the neighboring muscles. You may notice this area most when pushing big gears in a time trial, climbing in the saddle, or mountain biking. We'll go over a few pressure point techniques and stretches. Make sure to do one side, then the other. (Complete one side at a time.)

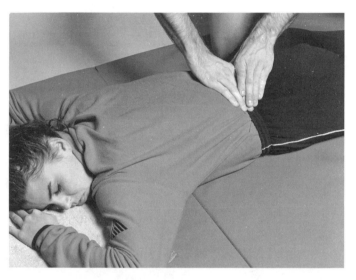

1. Grab the lower back, squeezing and rocking.

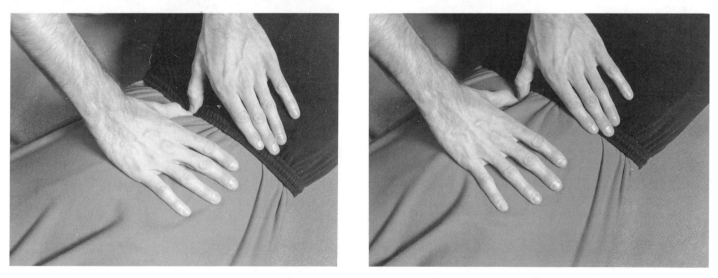

2. Apply direct pressure with your thumb to the muscle in the lower back that runs along the spine. Move back and forth over it (cross-fiber). Work a 3-4 inch area of the lower back.

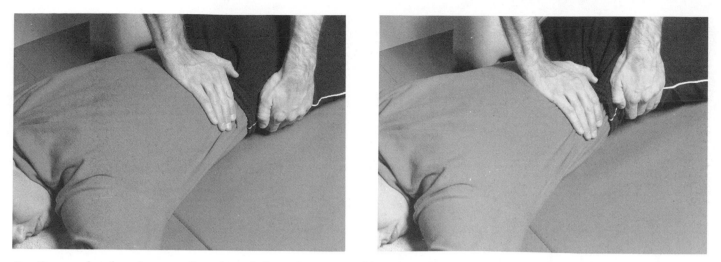

3. Stretch the lower back with what I call "the frame twister." Pull up on the hip bone (pelvis) with one hand while pushing down on the lower back muscle (not spine) with the other. Do both sides.

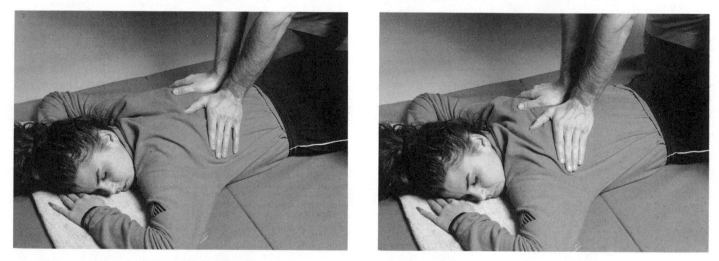

4. Direct pressure with your palms moving up the back. Your hands are beside the spine, not directly on it. Your hands are on muscle, not bone. Walk your way up the back with your hands.

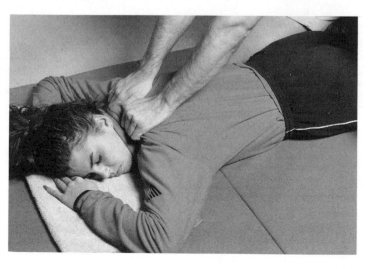

5. Grab the trapezius. Alternate squeezing.

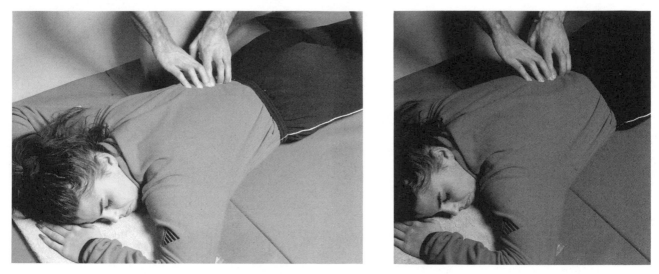

6. Crossfiber friction to the muscle along the side of the spine with your fingertips. Your fingers will twang across the muscle like guitar strings. Push and pull back and forth, moving along the entire spinae muscle.
Repeat on the other side.

7. Direct pressure to gluteals with your thumb or elbow.
(This is pictured in the pre-ride section, step 7.)

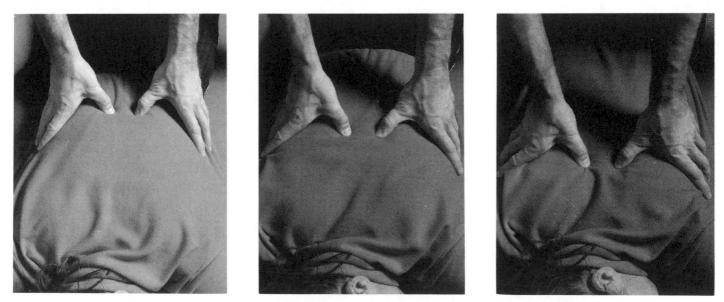

8. Direct pressure with your thumbs, inching your way up the spinae muscle. Hold for 10 to 20 seconds.
Move up a thumb width and repeat.

Finish with some hacking and jostling.

Lower back massage

❏ 1. Grab and squeeze small of lower back.

❏ 2. Direct pressure on lower back, straight down and from angle.

❏ 3. Frame-twister stretch.

❏ 4. Compressions with open hands on both sides of spine.

❏ 5. Squeeze trapezius.

❏ 6. Crossfiber to spinae muscle.

❏ 7. Direct pressure to glutes.

❏ 8. Direct pressure with thumbs to spinae muscle.

❏ 9. Hacking and/or jostling.

Static stretching

Stretching works together with massage in the care and maintenance of muscles. When done correctly, regular stretching can be an effective way to reduce muscle soreness. Stretching also increases muscle flexibility, which helps prevent injury.

Static stretching is the kind commonly recommended for cyclists. This involves moving into the maximum comfortable range of a particular muscle, holding for 30 to 60 seconds, relaxing, and repeating once or twice.

There are books on stretching that show many different stretches and give suggested routines. I include here 21 static stretches you can do on your own. After you've tried them for a while you'll learn which ones work best for you. You'll be able to develop routines that suit your needs.

The photos show the position of the stretch. The captions tell which muscles are involved and how to do the stretch. For quick reference you can just look at the photos. Don't forget to do both sides.

Use these guidelines in your stretching routine.

1. Never bounce. Hold your stretches for 30 to 60 seconds.

2. Move slowly and smoothly into the stretch and ease back out of it the same way.

3. Exhale into the stretch, then breathe normally.

4. Stay in your comfort zone. If you feel a twinge, pop, or sharp pain, STOP.

5. Muscles tend to stretch better when warmed up, so try to do your stretching after your ride or during breaks in other exercising. Ease into it gently on rest days or when you're just watching TV.

Gluteals and hips
Pull your knee toward the opposite shoulder.

Gluteals and hips
Cross your left leg over your right. Keeping your right leg flat on the floor, exhale and bend forward.

Gluteals and hips
Exhale and look over your shoulder while pushing back on your knee with your elbow.

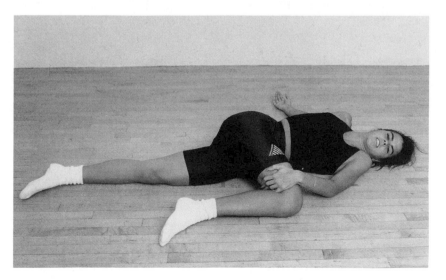

Gluteals and hips
Flex one knee toward your chest, grab it with one hand, and pull it across your body to the floor. Keep your shoulders flat on the floor.

Ankle and lower back
Exhale and slowly turn your ankle inward.

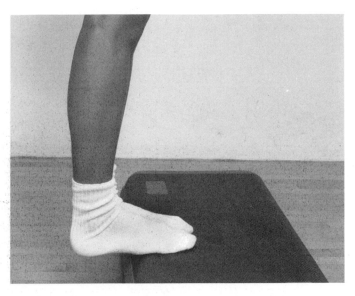

Achilles tendon
Lower your heels toward the floor.

Calf
Leaning against a wall, push your rear heel to the floor.

Achilles tendon and hamstring
Lower your head to the floor while stretching your extended foot.

**Hamstring group
and lower back**
Place your heel against the
inside of your opposite thigh.
Lean into the extended knee.

**Hamstring and
lower back**
Put your leg on an object
at a comfortable height.
Lean into your knee.

Lower back
Pull your knees toward your chest, raising your hips off the floor.

Lower back
Slowly lower your stomach between your legs.

Back
Keeping your lower body pointing forward and your feet flat on the floor, twist and stretch

Inner thigh
Bring the soles of your feet together as you pull them into your body. Push your knees toward the floor with your elbows

Lower back and inner thigh
Squat and push your knees out with your elbows. (Avoid this stretch if you've had knee injuries.)

Quadriceps
Laying on your side, pull your heel to your buttocks.

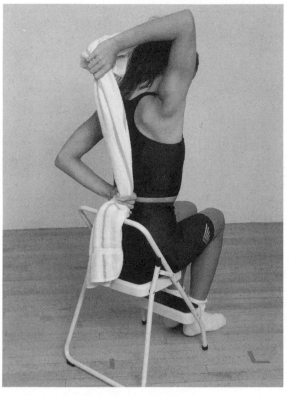

Triceps
Pull the towel with your lower hand to slowly stretch the triceps in your upper arm.

Quadriceps
Sit on your heels and slowly lean back.
(Avoid this stretch if you've had knee injuries.)

Neck
Pull your head toward your chest.
Keep your upper back on the floor.

Triceps
Pull your elbow behind your head.

PNF stretching

PNF (proprioceptive neuromuscular facilitation) is another kind of stretching that can help cyclists. It uses isometric contraction, meaning that the muscle is contracted without movement. This helps you achieve a deeper stretch than you can with static stretching. PNF stretching is a quick and effective way to gain flexibility without risk of injury.

The isometric contraction warms and sends blood to the muscle to be stretched. The muscle is mildly fatigued by this contraction and then is in better condition to relax and stretch further.

Here are the six steps in a PNF stretch:

1. Stretch the tight muscle as far as you can without pain.
   There is your starting point.

2. Have someone position himself or herself against you
   to act as resistance.

3. Isometrically contract against the person's resistance.
   The contraction should ease into 50% of maximum effort, always in
   a controlled manner. (Don't turn it into a contest of trying to move
   the other person.) Hold for a count of six.

4. Relax by taking a deep breath.

5. Under your own power, move the muscle into a deeper stretch.
   This is your new starting point.

6. Repeat the process three to five times or until you feel the stretch is
   complete and that you've stretched as far as possible. Be sure to
   communicate with your helper and let him or her know what you
   need (more or less resistance).

You should see a dramatic increase in range of motion in one session.

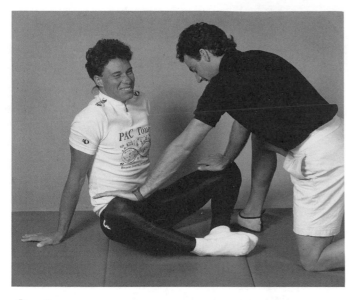

Groin

Contract the muscles of your groin and inner thigh against resistance for 6 seconds.

Relax. Take a deep breath. Move, unassisted, into a deeper stretch. This is the new starting point. Repeat 3-5 times.

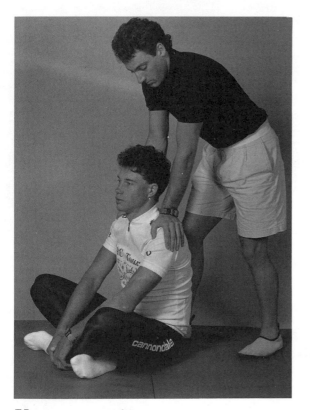

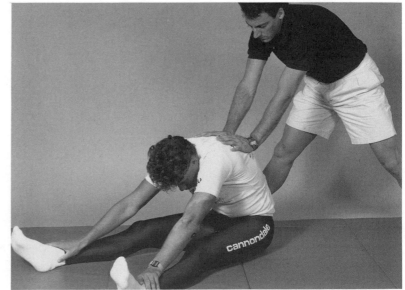

Upper trapezius

With your shoulders lowered, contract against resistance. Relax. Try to drop your shoulders lower. Repeat.

Back

Lean forward, then try to sit up against resistance. Relax. Bend deeper. Repeat.

Hamstring group

Contract your hamstring against resistance.

Relax. Take a deep breath. Move into a deeper stretch. Repeat.

For very tight hamstrings

Flex your knee. Place your heel against an immoveable object and push your heel toward the ground.
Relax. Pull your knee closer to your chest. Repeat.

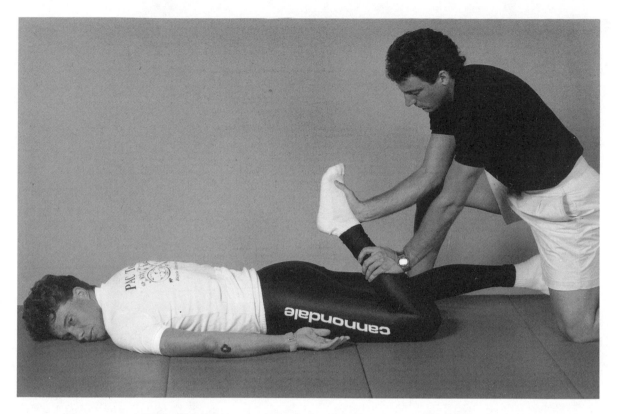

Quadriceps
Stretch your quads unassisted, then push against resistance. Relax. Move into a deeper stretch. Repeat.

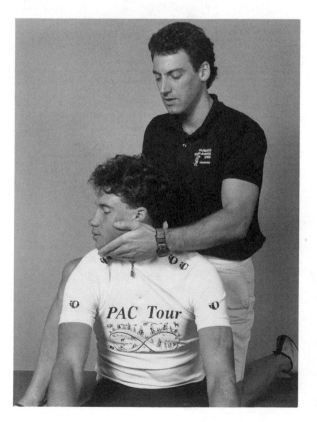

Neck
Turn your head as far to the side as possible, then turn back into resistance for 3 seconds. Relax. Take a deep breath. Turn into a deeper stretch. Repeat 3 times on each side. (This stretch is done for a shorter time and with fewer repetitions because the neck muscles can get strained more easily.)

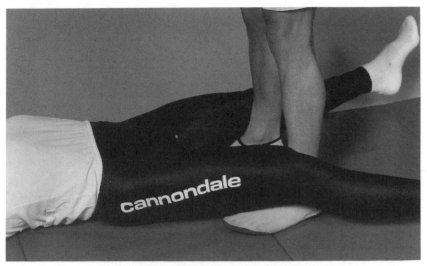

Inner thigh and groin
Lying on your back, contract against resistance. Relax. Move into a deeper stretch. Repeat.

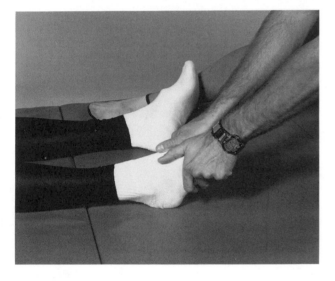

Shin (tibialis)
Stretch your ankle as straight as possible. Contract by pulling back against resistance. Relax. Stretch deeper. Repeat.

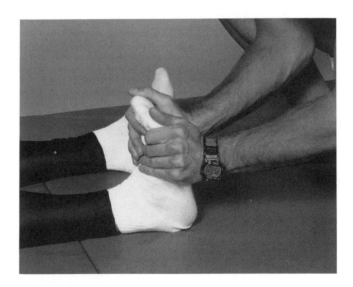

Calf
Pull your toes back, stretching your calf muscle. Push against resistance. Relax. Repeat.